RED ZONE

BLUE ZONE

RED ZONE

TURNING CONFLICT INTO OPPORTUNITY

BLUE ZONE

JAMES OSTERHAUS, PH.D.,
TODD HAHN, JOSEPH JURKOWSKI

Published by Familius LLC, www.familius.com

Familius books are available at special discounts for bulk purchases for sales promotions or
for family or corporate use. Special editions, including personalized covers, excerpts of exist-
ing books, or books with corporate logos, can be created in large quantities for special needs.
For more information, contact Premium Sales at 559-876-2170 or
email specialmarkets@familius.com

Library of Congress Catalog-in-Publication Data

2014959242

Paperback ISBN 978-1-939629-63-0
Hardcover ISBN 978-1-942672-77-7
Ebook ISBN 978-1-942672-04-3

Printed in the United States of America

Edited by Lindsay Sandberg
Cover design by David Miles
Book design by Lindsay Sandberg

2 0 1 4 9 5 9 2 4 2

First Edition

CONTENTS

PART ONE

Two of the coauthors, Jim and Todd, were once in prison together.

But only for a day.

Several years ago, we spent the day in Solano California State Prison in Vacaville, California, visiting a friend, David, who had been influenced by an earlier book we had written about how to thrive in—not just survive in—conflict.

David, now reintegrated into society outside prison walls, was an inmate and, at that time, was leading classes for other inmates on the topic of conflict resolution, largely based on our book.

He had invited us there to meet some of the hundreds of students he had led in exploring the principles of peacemaking.

On the appointed day, we went to the prison, passed through a gauntlet of metal detectors, and received our plastic whistles.

"Plastic whistles?" we asked.

"Yes," said the corrections officer, with a smile. "In the event that you get in a hostage situation or some such predicament, California state law says we can't negotiate for your release. If you sense trouble, blow your whistle as loudly as you can and hopefully an officer can get to you before things escalate."

We looked at each other.

It was too late to turn back. We walked into the heart of Solano Prison, and our worlds changed forever.

As we interacted with the men David was influencing, we saw that these people had internalized the principles of our book like no one else we had ever met.

These were former gang members—violent criminals, in many cases—people who had been excluded from society. And they were wise beyond belief. They brought tattered and underlined copies of our book to the meetings we attended, quoting passages and then teasing out the principles and applying them to their own lives and experiences.

They talked about their hopes for rejoining society— hopes and fears. They were determined that this time they would know how to head off the conflicts that, in many cases, had landed them in Solano. They got it, and as the day transpired, they became our teachers.

Conflict is common to everyone—parents, children, business leaders, public servants, pastors, inmates. We all face conflict. We can choose to ignore it, try to defeat it, or let it defeat us. We can try to simply survive it somehow. Or we can choose to see conflict for what it is—a revealer of our true selves and a rare opportunity for growth and change—and leverage it as an experience that will help us to thrive.

We've seen these principles play out in therapy sessions and in boardrooms, in the halls of churches and in agencies of the federal government, on playgrounds and in penitentiaries. We've seen men and women learn how to embrace conflict, see it as their ally, and learn to lead others wisely and well. This new perspective changes everything, just as our lives were changed that day at Solano.

We offer this story, and these principles and exercises, in the hope that you will learn to thrive through conflict as well, and that all our lives will be better because of it.

CHAPTER ONE

CONFLICTED BEGINNINGS

Michael O'Reilly's family emigrated from Ireland when he was a teenager, and he later worked his way through college in the Chicago area. He married and settled in the suburb of Elizabethton. Two years later, his first son, Bob, was born.

Michael had always been good with his hands and his brain, and he became a highly respected owner of a small plumbing company. But his ambitions were bigger than a few employees and the residential trade. He was able to beg and borrow enough money to first found a plumbing supply company and to later purchase a firm that manufactured those supplies. The firm was located in Massachusetts, and Michael moved the family there when Bob was sixteen years old. Due to Michael's hard work and business savvy, the company prospered, as did the O'Reilly family.

Michael had always assumed that Bob would join the family business and, after college, he did. Bob worked his way through the ranks—Michael did not believe in nepotism—and eventually it was clear that Bob would succeed his father as CEO, though the transition wasn't going as smoothly as Bob might have hoped. The plan had been for Bob to become acting CEO, the CEO-designate, and for Michael to step into a senior adviser role until Bob adjusted to his new responsibilities. Bob was now CEO, but each new day at the office proved to him that Michael had not stepped down enough.

THE DAILY CONFLICT

Even though he had spent most of his life in western Massachusetts, Bob O'Reilly had never gotten used to the cold. And this February afternoon was bitingly chilly.

Bob turned his coat collar up against the chill as he made his way across the parking lot toward his office at O'Reilly Plumbing Manufacturers. His mind was filled with the question of the succession plan and his need to establish himself as the man in charge if the company was going to progress.

Even though Michael said all the right things, he had a commanding presence and hard-won respect from his employees. It was clear to thirty-five-year-old Bob that many of his team of three hundred employees still believed that the seventy-year-old patriarch was the man in charge.

Worse, Bob believed that his father was doing things to contribute to this sense. He had a tendency to question his son's decisions in meetings, and sometimes made joking side comments about "the way we always used to do things around here."

The plan had been for Michael to serve in an advisory capacity for eighteen months after Bob got the title of CEO-designate, and, under normal circumstances, Bob would have gritted his teeth and waited the old man out. But the last eighteen months had been the most difficult in the firm's history. The downturn in the US economy pushed home builders who bought the firm's products to go out of business and home owners to put off plumbing upgrades. On top of losing customers, several of the firm's biggest competitors had begun outsourcing manufacturing functions or even moving their operations to Mexico, where labor was a fraction of the cost. Truth be told, the company was on the rocks.

Bob had scheduled a meeting with his father for this morning to present the drastic steps he believed the firm needed to take. He walked into his own office a few minutes early to gather his thoughts before he had to walk down the hall to Michael's office.

Bob sank into his office chair, breathed a deep sigh, and ran his fingers through his hair. It had been a rough couple of years; The conflict with his father. The company's struggles. His marriage of ten years ending in divorce. "At least there were no kids," he reminded himself for the thousandth time, but the silver lining sounded hollow even to him.

He reached into his briefcase, pulled out a legal pad, and once again reviewed his notes for the meeting with his father.

First, the challenges:

- The economic downturn, which showed no signs of abating
- The resultant cash-flow crunch
- Competitors finding cheaper, often foreign, means of production
- An uncertainty within the company about who was really in charge

Next, Bob's proposed solutions:

- Significant layoffs in a company which had never let people go for financial reasons
- Exploration of moving some of the company's operations offshore
- Clear communication from the executive ranks that Bob is now firmly in charge and that Michael has a lessened role

It promised to be a difficult meeting. Michael was the prototypical feisty, dyed-in-the-wool Irish immigrant. He had achieved success through hard work over long hours, risk-taking, an aversion to compromise, and command-and-control management. He contrasted this rough exterior by caring deeply for his team, keeping employees on even when times were tough.

Bob anticipated that his father would push back ferociously against all three of his proposed solutions. But a crisis was coming, and the conflict could no longer be avoided.

Bob steeled himself, got up from his desk, stuffed the legal pad back into his briefcase, and walked down the hall to Michael's office.

From behind Michael's door, Bob heard the sound of laughter as another man emerged with a wave of his hand. Bob stiffened a bit when he saw who had been in the office with his father. David Thomas was a fifteen-year veteran of the company, heading up floor operations. He was, in many ways, Michael's best friend in the company and was considered to be privy to the former CEO's thoughts and intentions. Bob had often felt resentful of the man, even though he could come up with no good reason. His performance was stellar, and he said all the right things about the transfer of company leadership to Bob. But Bob had a feeling—a gut instinct—that David wished that the old man were still in charge and preferred Bob's father's way of doing things.

Bob pushed David out of his mind for the moment, strode into his father's office, and took a seat across the desk. "Hey, Dad. Ready to dive in?"

Michael laughed loudly. "Wow, we're full of piss and vinegar today, aren't we, son? Sure you don't want some coffee first?"

"No, thanks," Bob replied. "Got some pretty important stuff to get into today. Can we get going?"

"Sure, son," Michael said with a wave of his hand and a chuckle. "But you know, you might want to think about being a little softer when you call meetings to order, you know? You can get away with being Mr. Serious with me because I'm your old man, but you want to make sure you don't alienate everyone else around here."

"OK, Dad, whatever," Michael said impatiently. "Here's the deal. We're still a few days away from getting the first-quarter financials, but we both know they're bad. As I see it, this economy is not getting better anytime soon if we do what we've always done. The housing industry is not going to come back for at least a few years, meaning demand for our product line is going to be, at best, flat. We can't compete for the few customers who are left because all of our competitors have us beat on price point. It's a bad situation, getting worse by the day. I think we have to be prepared to take some drastic measures."

He paused for breath, noting that he was speaking fast. Determined to look and sound like a measured leader, he forced himself to slow down.

"Look, here's the deal, Dad. I am proposing—insisting, really—that we take a two-pronged approach. First, we have to do something neither of us wants to do: we have to make significant layoffs. There's not enough work, there's no promise of more work, and I lie awake at night worrying about cash flow."

Bob noticed that his father's face reddened and he was about to speak, so Bob pressed on quickly.

"Hang on; let me finish. We need to cut deepest in the areas where we can outsource or move our operations. We should focus our Massachusetts operations on sales, marketing, and strategy, doing anything we can to identify and cultivate new markets. We need to consider sending all of our manufacturing operations somewhere with cheaper labor and production costs. This means, of course, that we will have to cut people that we don't want to cut, like David."

"Stop, stop!" Michael exclaimed. "You've got to understand that everything you're saying—absolutely everything—is a non-starter. That is not how we built this company. We don't lay people off; we take care of our people. And as good as this country has been to me, we sure as hell don't send work to Mexico! No, no; I am telling you we are not going to do any of that. Or, rather, if we do, it will be over my dead body!"

Michael's temper was legendary and had intimidated many through the years, but Bob was used to it and was pretty intense himself. Plus, he had some anxiety and frustration built up.

"OK. I should have said we need to take a three-pronged approach. And you, Dad, are the third prong. In case you have forgotten, I am the acting CEO now. You are a senior adviser, and the clock is running out on that, quite frankly. I love you, but you are hamstringing and undermining me. You constantly tell me that I need to do things just like you did, manage the company like you managed it, and, in general, be the executive and the man you are!"

Bob had the feeling he should stop, but he was committed to and vested in his emotion at this point. "Dad, I respect you both as a man and as a businessman, but you are killing me. We don't live in the days when you built this company, when housing boomed, recessions were predictable and short-lived, foreign competition was minimal, and companies could promise lifelong employment. We just don't!

"Times have changed, and business has to change; that's why I am leading this company now and you are stepping into a well-deserved retirement. But you're not letting me get the traction I need. You think I don't know that when I explain a decision in a room full of people, everyone glances at you to see if you are on board? And that if you're not—and, oh, we know when you're not—they're not on board either?

"Dad, this can't go on. Not only do we need to implement my strategy of layoffs and operations relocation, but we need you to get behind me and make it clear that I am the leader here now!"

"Bob, you are out of line!" Michael shouted. "The business principles I used to build this place still work and always will. They are timeless! And the people principles are even more important. Not only are you making rash decisions on the business end, but you are also undermining the people principles I built into the DNA of this place. I'm starting to become afraid that you are going to run this place into the ground and destroy my legacy!"

Breathing hard, standing now, both men paused for a long moment, staring at one another.

Michael exhaled, sank back in his chair, and waved wearily. "Ah, I don't mean all of that. Not all of it. But you have to pull it together, boy-o. There's a lot at stake in this place, for all of us. For me, it's my life's work."

Michael spun his chair around to look at the window, breaking his gaze with Bob. "Plus, if there is one person here we can't lay off, it's David."

Bob felt his face flush and he started to speak, but Michael cut him off.

"Wait, wait. There's a story you need to know. A story I probably should have told you a while ago."

CHAPTER TWO

THE REAL QUESTION

"What do you mean, a story?" Bob asked. "What possible story could mean a man is layoff-proof? Let's be honest, he's a decent floor manager. But in the last few years he's become more of a floating guru around here. You seem to have let him become an executive without a portfolio, able to stick his nose wherever he wants. I've never been a fan of that. We need people who execute around here, not Yodas."

"First of all, he's way better than decent, and you know that. And second of all, he is a guy with an invaluable ability to size up a situation, see the underlying issues, and offer wise counsel," Michael replied. "But let's leave that alone for now. Let me tell you the story."

Bob nodded impatiently, so Michael continued.

"You know that David and I were in high school together when I was a senior and he was a freshman. We both played football and were teammates for that one year. Pretty good friends, but not bosom buddies. Then we lost touch until about fifteen years ago, when I asked him to come to work here.

"There's no easy way to say this, Bob. David spent twenty-five years in jail for second-degree murder."

Bob's throat went dry—which didn't matter much, because he was too shocked to speak.

Michael continued. "After high school, he fell in with the wrong crowd and gradually became part of that wrong crowd. Lots of drinking and carousing, involvement in what passed for gangs back then. A little violence—at first just street ruffian kind of stuff. David was always sort of a half-hearted bad guy. I always thought he was looking for acceptance more than he wanted to do anyone harm.

"And then there was a really bad night. David and his friends got into a confrontation in the street. David actually had a handgun. Stupid move; trying to impress some girl. He doesn't really remember what happened, but the gun went off. In his hand. Long story short, the other guy died the next day. David and his friends had run away, but they soon ratted him out. He went down for second-degree murder, served his time, and was released."

Bob had found his voice. "You're kidding me, right?" Michael simply spread his hands apart in an *I got nothing* gesture.

Bob got to his feet slowly, but with his fury quickening.

"We have a murderer on our payroll. A violent criminal in a position of influence. A freaking 'elder statesman' in our family firm. Somebody who took a human life was with us at Thanksgiving last year. Works down the hall from me. Is a potential danger to everyone in this facility. And you allowed this? You encouraged this? And somehow never saw fit to tell me?"

"Two things, Bob," said Michael. "First, he admitted his guilt, was a model prisoner, and paid his debt to society. Second, I probably should have told you. I didn't because I figured you would react this way. So I was right and wrong all at once. It is what it is.

"One more thing," Michael continued. "He came to me asking for a job after his release. I felt the same way about convicted felons then as you feel now. But because we had been teammates back in the day, I felt that I owed him the courtesy of an interview. I looked him in the eye, listened to him talk, took his measure. I believed him when he said that he was a changed man. I gave him an entry-level job and never had cause to regret my decision for a moment. Again, I should have told you, maybe, but it is what it is."

Bob's head was spinning. "No, it is what it was. You do see what has to happen, right? He has to go now. Forget planned layoffs—we can't have a guy like that on our payroll. He's gone today. You have got to be kidding me."

"Not as long as I am still employed here, he isn't fired," Michael shot back. "I gave him a second chance, and he made the most of it. He has served this company and this family well.

He could be an invaluable asset to you as CEO if you would let him. Plus, he's had only fifteen years to save for retirement, and who is going to give a sixty-something felon a job in this economy?"

"That's not my problem," Bob snapped with barely contained fury. "You always preached self-reliance and personal responsibility to me, Dad. David pulled the trigger. He made his choice. And now I am making mine. He's gone. Done. Today."

Michael spoke with an odd chill in his voice. "I'd like to see you try it, Bob."

Bob's mind raced. In a moment, he saw this conversation for what it was. A test. A test of his manhood. A test of his leadership. A test of his relationship with his father. And a test over who was running the family firm.

He knew what he needed to do. What he was going to do. But he had to make sure that he made all the right moves, that he marginalized his father's influence over the future of the company once and for all. This was a crucible moment.

"OK, Dad," he said after a pause. "I'm going to do one thing, as a show of respect to you. I'm calling David into my office. I'm giving him five minutes to tell me why he thinks he deserves to stay here. And once he doesn't give me a good answer, I'm cutting him loose." He turned and walked toward the office door, glanced over his shoulder, and saw Michael reaching for his phone.

Bob spun around. "Don't you dare call him. I'm handling this. Stay out of it." He left the room.

AN AWKWARD CONVERSATION

Fifteen minutes later, David Thomas knocked on Bob's half-open office door. "You wanted to see me, boss?"

"Yep, come in. Have a seat. This is a hard conversation, but it seems today I am in the business of having hard conversations. I'll cut to the chase. My dad told me about your crime and your imprisonment. I was shocked, to put it mildly. Shocked that no one had told me, that you thought it was OK that I not know. And shocked that we have someone with your track record in our employ. Your position is no longer available to you, but I wanted to give you a chance to explain yourself."

David puffed his cheeks out and blew. "Boy. Wow. Um, well, needless to say, it's true. I committed a crime in my youth. Check that—'in my youth' sounds like an excuse. I committed a crime. I took another human life, and not a day goes by that I don't feel sorry for that and for the pain I caused so many people. I deserved to go to prison. It was the hardest experience of my life.

"But it changed me, Bob. Changed me for the better. I came out of there determined to make a positive difference in the lives of others. I've tried my level best to be a positive difference-maker for this company for the last fifteen years. I have no excuse, no justification. I just have a story; hopefully, one that will end better than it began."

David seemed about to continue, but thought better of it and stopped, inviting Bob's response with a glance.

"I hope that's right, David," Bob said. "I hope you've changed your life. I wish you well, but I can't have you working for my company. We have a reputation in this community. I have a responsibility to protect my employees. Most of all, I have a reputation to uphold as the CEO of this company.

"Look, I know the relationship you have with my dad, and that's fine. But you don't have that with me. And you never will, especially now that I know this. I have to lead this firm my way, not my dad's way. I have to do the right thing by my own lights. I have to step up. It's time for me to step up."

Recognizing that he was talking more about himself than he had intended—and not quite sure why—Bob stopped.

David smiled at him kindly, not exactly the response Bob was expecting.

"Look, Bob. I gotta tell you, I respect you stepping up. I know this has been hard for you. I believe you want to do the right thing. And if letting me go is the right thing, I respect that, too. I'll go. But if you will let me offer you one last piece of unsolicited advice . . . "

Suddenly weary and thinking that the hardest part of the conversation was over, Bob simply nodded.

"Bob, you have to make sure that what you believe is the right thing in the moment is in fact the right thing. Look, you have all the power in this company, and you have for the past year. And you can exercise that power. But if you fire me, if you fire all of us—and I know you have to be thinking of layoffs—is that going to get you what you want? And by 'what you want,' I mean is this going to solve the problems you're facing?"

Bob stared at David blankly, not really processing what he was saying.

"OK, Bob; you've made your decision. I have enjoyed working with you, and I wish this company all the best. I am going to go clean out my office, if that's OK with you."

David pulled his lanky frame out of his chair, stepped across the carpet, and stretched out his hand to Bob. Still surprised at the gentleness and acceptance in David's response, Bob shook his now ex-employee's hand.

After David left, Bob shook his head, trying to clear the cobwebs. It had been a whirlwind of a morning. He was sure he had done the right thing. It was the right thing morally, and it was also necessary to put his stamp on the company. So why didn't he feel better about things?

After all, he had won a key battle with his dad, going one up and setting the precedent for the tough decisions to come. "I'm just tired," he reasoned. "Just really tired. I'll get a good night's sleep. That's what I need."

A NAGGING QUESTION

But Bob didn't get a wink of sleep that night. In spite of his weariness, he found himself staring at the ceiling at three in the morning, thinking. Well, more wondering than thinking.

There had been a whole lot about his conversation
with David that had puzzled him—David's non-defensive
response, for one thing. In spite of losing his job as a sixty-something convicted felon, David had appeared to be
remarkably free of anxiety.

And another thing—David's comment about power.
Bob experienced being in a pitched battle for power every
day. Battling against the old man, against the declining
economy, against competition that was lowering its costs—
and, hence, its prices—and against the intense weight of the
historic success of the company. Sure, he had the title of
CEO, but, in many ways, he was convinced that his dad was
still the real power broker.

One more thing—David's odd comment about Bob's decisions in solving the problems he was facing. That really
made no sense. Solving problems was precisely what he
was doing. He had identified the key issues—Michael's
hanging on to power, stronger competition, an economic
slowdown—and had come up with the right solutions, in
order: taking a stand and stepping up as a leader, beginning
layoffs, and moving operations offshore.

The best he could tell, Bob had provided the perfect solution for each of the company's three main problems. All he
had to do was execute and get rid of the obstacles in his way.

So exactly what "problem" was David referring to?

His brain truly fried now, Bob rolled over and began
anew to fight the power of sleeplessness. He lost.

SETTING THE HOOK

By the next morning, David's questions were driving Bob nuts. When he thought about it later, he would figure that the lack of sleep made him act in such an uncharacteristically impulsive way. Because he did something bizarre: he called David and invited him to lunch, supposedly to talk about his severance package. But Bob's real agenda was different.

They met at Smokey's, a seafood joint renowned for its crab cakes. They didn't rival the crab cakes of Maryland's Chesapeake Bay, but they were delicious. Over plates of the delectable cakes and mounds of coleslaw and French fries, Bob outlined a relatively generous severance plan for David.

David agreed readily, the check came, and Bob paid up. And then lingered. For a long time.

After a while, David smiled across the table at Bob and said, "Do you mind if I ask you a question?"

"Yeah, sure," Bob replied.

"Well, Bob, in all the time I have known you, you have never lingered after the check was paid, alternating silence and small talk. Usually you are brushing crab cake crumbs off your shirt as you rush out the door. So I have to ask you—is there anything you want to talk about?"

As he considered his response, Bob had a strange sense that what he said was going to define a fork in the road in his career. And he had no idea why. What he should do was stay one up, thank the dismissed employee one more time, and get back to work. But he didn't.

"Well, yeah, David. I do," Bob blurted out. "A couple things, really. One is that I can't believe how calm and not anxious you were yesterday. I don't really want to talk about that, because I am afraid you are going to credit it to Jesus or Zen or something, and I don't want to go there. But I do want to ask about two things.

"First, I don't get what you meant by wondering if my decisions are going to solve our problems. Of course they will! That's what leaders do: identify problems and either use their expertise to solve them or find the right expert and let him do his thing. You lose revenue; you make cuts. Your competition lowers production costs and underprices you; you copy their methods. You're in a power struggle; you fight till you come out on top and insist on your priorities. Problem, meet solution.

"And second, you really have me stumped with your comment about me having all the power. I know you and Dad are friends, David, and he is my father, so I don't want to slam him, but come on! You and I both know he still holds the real levers of power in this organization. You don't think I know that every time I state a course of action, everyone in the room looks at him to see if he buys in?"

David was silent for what, to Bob, was an uncomfortable amount of time. Finally, he spoke.

"I think, Bob, you are asking some profound questions. I have some very specific thoughts on the topic of problems and solutions. But I know you have a very limited amount of time, and I am picking up that the question that is really bugging you is the one about power. Am I right?"

Bob nodded, so David continued.

Except "continued" is too mild a word. What David did was speak a sentence that dropped like a bombshell in Bob's heart and head and would eventually change the way he saw everything.

"Bob, here's the deal. Ever since you became CEO-designate, you have always had the power. And, by the way, every time you state a course of action, *you* look at your dad to see if he buys in as well."

CHAPTER THREE

RED ZONE, BLUE ZONE

Needless to say, David's comment stunned Bob and struck him to his core. He pondered the thought long after leaving Smokey's. How in the world was it possible that he could be one of the employees deferring to his dad? Impossible! As a matter of fact, it was this deferral that was driving him crazy; it would be the very last behavior he would be guilty of. Or so he reasoned.

But he couldn't let go of the sense that there was something to what David was saying. And he couldn't deny that David had conducted himself with class and dignity and had said some undeniably wise things. It was also true that Bob was beginning to question whether his decision to summarily terminate David had been wise or just. Upon reflection, he had to acknowledge that it would be difficult for David to find much-needed employment. And, to be sure, David had performed his job with distinction for the company. Furthermore, Bob was convinced that David was an honest broker, not an unbiased fan of the father who has long knives out for the son.

So, intrigued by David's words and feeling more than a little guilty about his own behavior, Bob arrived at a novel plan. He would keep David on retainer as a personal consultant. Paid his previous salary, David would not work in the plant or in the corporate offices, but he would meet regularly with Bob to talk through issues related to the succession plan and to the company's struggles.

Bob invited David to his home office the next day.

"Bob, I am honored and delighted that you trust me in this way," David said when Bob leaned back in his office chair, having described the proposal. "I am glad to serve as a consultant to you. But I don't need any money. I will do it for no cost."

"David, how can you do that?" asked Bob, startled. "You were making a good salary, and it is going to be hard for you to find work given your . . . um . . . past."

"Bob, I am a man of simple needs, and I have been quite fortunate in some investments," David replied. "It would be my joy to serve you and the company that has treated me so well."

"Are you sure? That's a lot to ask of anyone."

"Yes, I'm sure. In the course of my life, especially my post-prison life, I have been served by many, and their service has helped me a great deal. I am delighted to offer anything I can to you and to your company."

Bob nodded. "OK, here's what I am thinking. We meet once a week with a set agenda, but I would love to be able to call you between meetings if something arises. How does that sound?"

David smiled. "Bob, I want this to be as comfortable for you as possible, so that is fine with me. But I have found that leadership crises, such as the one the company finds itself in now, rarely lend themselves to carefully planned agendas. Things simply move too fast and change too quickly. I will be available to you when you need me." David paused. "By the way, there is something I am wondering."

"Sure. What is it?" Bob replied.

"Do you have a few moments now?" David asked.

Bob nodded, so David continued. "I'd like to share a couple of very important concepts with you that I think may help you understand the tension you are feeling in the company over your succession to CEO and—if I may say so—the tension you are experiencing with your father."

All at once, Bob felt defensive. But he did his best to mask it. He shifted in his seat and cleared his throat.

"Like I said, David, I am eager to glean your insights. But I'd feel most comfortable if we confined our discussions to professional matters and didn't get into family concerns." He smiled in a way he thought was winning.

"Bob, I'm going to take a risk here and push back a little," David replied. "I want what is best for you and for this company, so I am going to say the hard things that I think are true, even if that causes you to end our arrangement. The fact of the matter is that there is no way to separate the tensions between you and your father from the dilemmas in which the company finds itself."

Bob's jaw tensed, but he didn't interrupt, so David continued.

"I don't pretend to be a family therapist, but I do believe in the connectedness of things. Your relationship with your dad profoundly affects and influences the direction and future of the company. I don't ask that you buy into what I am saying now, but that you at least promise to suspend disbelief for a time."

"I don't buy what you're saying," said Bob, who stood and walked to his mini-fridge to grab two water bottles, handing one to David and placing the other on his own desk, within reach. "But I don't really want to argue about it now. I'd rather you just plow ahead and talk about the important concepts you mentioned."

David smiled, probably recognizing Bob's discomfort. "Sure, Bob—that I will do.

"Here's the first one. Now, brace yourself. It won't be easy for you to hear, at first. The first concept is that you are the problem."

Bob rolled his eyes, defensive and suspicious. "Oh boy, I should have guessed. The old man put you up to this, didn't he? You've got to be kidding me, David. You are parroting his line that my leadership is the cause of all of the company's struggles."

"No, no, Bob," David interjected. "You've got to hear me say two things. First, although your father and I are close friends, in the matter of my consulting with you, you have my promise of confidentiality. I'm not taking sides. I really do want the best for the company and all of its employees, including you, and I will offer the best counsel I can.

"Second, when I said that you are the problem, it had nothing to do—necessarily—with your business leadership. The fact is that you are in conflict. Conflict with your father and inner conflict as you try to figure out what is best for the company. What I am saying is that when we face conflict, the first place to look is at ourselves. Which is, of course, the last place we are inclined to look.

"When we are in conflict, almost every time, there is as much or more conflict in ourselves as there is between us and another person. Resolving the conflict doesn't happen when we convince or defeat the other person; it begins to happen when we take the gutsy step of looking inside of ourselves and being willing to ask ourselves tough questions."

"That's a tough pill to swallow, David," Bob said when the older man paused for a moment. "Look, I get that I have some inner turmoil—call it conflict if you want. But I can't buy that every conflict is in me. Sometimes people are just plain wrong, me included. How would we ever get anything done if everyone just navel-gazed every time they got crossways with someone else?"

"Oh, it may be true that the other person is wrong," said David, shrugging. "Or that both of you are partially wrong. But that's not my point. What I am saying is that when I am in conflict, there is something in me that is deeply unsettled, regardless of the circumstances that precipitated the conflict. And that it's worth asking myself why."

"OK, I can buy that, at least on a provisional basis," said Bob. "So, what's your next magic concept?"

"There's no magic here, my friend," David laughed. "Just some hard-won wisdom, I believe." David opened his water bottle and took a drink before continuing.

"The second concept is connected to the first one. You are looking to take the company through some profound changes. The company as a whole and all of its employees must change. And you must change as well, Bob. So it's worth reflecting on change.

"There are different kinds of change. I want to get into this with you later, but, for now, let me introduce the distinction between tactical and transformational change.

"Tactical change occurs when it is obvious what needs to be done. You have snow in your driveway; you shovel it. Your hard drive crashes; you call the company's IT gurus. Tactical change simply requires bringing in the right expert or using the right expertise.

"Transformational change, on the other hand, is change at the level of belief, values, and behavior. It is hard work to lead transformational change, because it will require very different behaviors and even beliefs. It will actually alter the structure of the work environment and the relationships that exist there.

"But here is the secret, Bob: transformational change is where the real work of leadership takes place. And given the challenges the company faces, it is transformational change which you must lead."

Bob was quiet, seemingly lost in thought, so David thought he should clarify further. Glancing around, he saw what he needed.

"Hey, Bob, can I use the whiteboard you have in the corner? OK, thanks."

David rummaged in a package of dry erase markers until he found three particular colors and waved them so Bob could see them.

"Let me tie these ideas of conflict and change together visually, since I know you Irish guys learn best with pretty pictures," said David with a chuckle and a wink.

"I call this the difference between living in the Blue Zone and in the Red Zone."

He picked up a black marker from the whiteboard's tray and drew a vertical line from the top of the board to the bottom. Then he took a blue marker and wrote "Blue Zone" at the top of the left column and followed suit by writing "Red Zone" with a red marker at the top of the right column.

"OK, the basic idea is this: when we are in conflict, we can choose to respond in one of two ways. The first way is from the Blue Zone. The Blue Zone is where you maintain professionalism and you keep your emotional cool. You can tell when someone is in the Blue Zone by several behaviors they demonstrate."

David jotted a phrase at the top of the left column.

Focus on efficiency and effectiveness.

"This creates a workplace where everyone shows up to do their job, they have the right tools, and they are motivated to do good work. They're not distracted by drama and political intrigue. The workplace has a buzz, an energy."

David wrote another phrase just below the first.

Structures of the organization are closely monitored and respected.

"What this means," David continued, "is that stuff like performance reviews, goal-setting and follow-up evaluation, and reporting structures—the often-ignored guts of an organization—are actually respected. This is all about accountability, but not the kind of soul-crushing accountability that is really micromanagement. The truth is, Bob, accountability is built on trust. And when everyone agrees on standards and expectations, trust flourishes."

David wrote another phrase.

Business issues are the top priority.

"When a business has a clear sense of mission, strong and vibrant core values, and a winning strategy, it has a chance to succeed. But only a chance. If those core business issues are not seen as the first thing—if other issues like personal rivalries or clawing for territory are allowed to take top place—the workplace becomes a miserable environment. I think you might be feeling some of that, Bob."

David sat down and looked intently into Bob's eyes. "So, to recap," he said. "The Blue Zone is the place of emotional health and professional focus. Is this making sense so far, Bob?"

The younger man thought for a moment.

"I think so, David. I get the difference between tactical and transformational change. And I understand that an organization that focuses on set goals and values is probably a great place to work. I mean, who doesn't believe that? What I don't get is how we can get so far off course, where virtually everyone forgets or just plain refuses to hold to those values."

"Well, Bob," said David, "The answer to that is all about the Red Zone. Can I continue by explaining that?" Bob nodded, so David wrote a phrase in red at the top of the right column.

Focus on feelings more than results.

"This is the polar opposite of a focus on efficiency and effectiveness. Feelings matter more than results. And while there is no doubt that feelings are important to human beings, when they become the focus, they are an enormous distraction. People are confused about where their personal and professional boundaries are, and this paralyzes everyone. The organization gets off base because everyone has taken their eye off the ball."

"I get that!" Bob interrupted. "That's what it feels like now at the company. We have all of these strategic and competitive issues to deal with, and my dad just wants to hark back to the good old days!"

"There may be something to what you say, Bob," David replied. "But remember that the focus here needs to be not in pointing fingers, but in looking inward, even though it's hard. The Red Zone is all about blame-shifting."

There was an uncomfortable pause before David plowed on.

No common standards and no way of monitoring performance and behavior.

"In the Red Zone, no one gets it. They don't get what they are supposed to be doing, they don't get what counts as good work in the organization, and they don't get where the ethical lines are drawn. So this results in all kinds of confusion and the thing that confusion always leads to—anxiety. And when you are not sure what you are supposed to be doing and you are feeling a high level of anxiety, the natural reaction is to lash out at others. So you have these endless cycles of blame-shifting, political maneuvering, and recrimination.

"One more thing, and then I'm done." David wrote a final line in red:

People expect the organization to be a family, and they assume family roles.

"Bob, this happens in most organizations. But where it really becomes an issue is in family-owned businesses, because the lines really get blurred. Think about it—you are the successor to your dad. The business boundaries and the family boundaries are understandably going to be really hard to keep clear.

"What makes this such a challenge is that families and healthy workplaces do some of the same things—they provide a sense of relational satisfaction, meaning, and purpose. But they are radically different in other ways. Families are designed to nurture, train, and develop their members to face a chaotic world, which will have only one constant—the family itself! In healthy families, the members are always there for each other, regardless.

"Businesses are very different. They can't do some of the things that families do. There is no 'forever' in business. Sometimes colleagues have to separate due to a change in life, disagreement, or poor performance. A healthy person subordinates the needs of his job to those of his family and draws a bright line between the two. It's when this boundary is unclear that confusion, misunderstanding, and anger emerge. And I see this happening with you and your dad.

"This confusion also comes in when people adopt family roles in the workplace—a female manager becomes a 'mother hen,' fiercely protecting her brood. A male manager becomes a father figure. A young man becomes the wayward younger brother. When we start to enact family roles in the workplace, our focus and energy suffer."

The whiteboard now looked like this:

BLUE ZONE	RED ZONE
Focus on efficiency and effectiveness.	Focus on feelings more than results.
Structures of the organization are closely monitored and respected.	No common standards and no way of monitoring performance and behavior.
Business issues are the top priority.	People in the organization assume family roles.

David paused and looked at Bob for a long moment. "Doing OK?" he asked.

Bob thought for a bit before replying. "Yes, I think so. It's a lot to take in."

David laughed. "I know. So let me try to sum up, and I'll let you get to the rest of your day.

"Bottom line: when people in an organization are operating in the Blue Zone, they are focused on the right things, with clear standards and expectations of behavior and interaction, and they are emotionally healthy. But when they are in the Red Zone—driven by personal, emotional, and unprofessional motives—work feels like a battlefield, with petty jealousies and annoyances, recriminations, shifting alliances, and Machiavellian political machinations.

"Blue Zone equals fun. Red Zone equals no fun."

David sat back down and looked into Bob's eyes. "I'm not sure you're having much fun these days, are you?"

Bob laughed bitterly. "Fun? Um, no. I'm not even sure I can imagine that. But, look; I need to think about all this Red Zone/Blue Zone stuff more. And I also need to get moving. How do you suggest we proceed?"

David nodded. "OK, right. Before we meet again, I want you to think about three questions—really think about them. And we can discuss your answers next time." He wrote on the board again.

- Am I more of a Red Zone or Blue Zone executive?
- What are examples of Red Zone and Blue Zone behavior I have demonstrated this week?
- Do I tend to focus more on tactical or transformational change when I encounter an obstacle?

David moved toward the door of Bob's study, pausing before taking his leave.

"The thing, Bob, is that those are tough questions. They require more than simple answers. They require taking an intensely honest look inside yourself. It's work that not every business executive can do. But I think that your success and that of the company we both love may well hinge on your being able to do that hard, inner work. I believe you can do it. I really do. All right; I'll let you get to it. I'll show myself out."

And with that, David was gone.

CHAPTER FOUR

THE REAL PROBLEM

Bob woke up the next day decidedly *not* thinking about the Blue Zone and the Red Zone. Though he had been intrigued by David's concepts, his sense was that today he had bigger fish to fry. At the top of the agenda was a meeting with his CFO, Ted, to go over the last quarter's financials.

At eight o'clock sharp, Ted knocked on Bob's office door with dark smudges under his eyes.

"Bob, I didn't sleep a wink last night. I have some tough news."

And with that, Bob leaned back in his chair to listen as the CFO launched into a dire presentation of the company's financial state. In the last few months, the company had faced declining demand, soaring costs, and a record loss. The company was not leaking; it was hemorrhaging.

After twenty minutes, Ted's voice trailed off. "I could keep going, but I'm pretty sure you get the picture, Bob."

Bob felt more tired than he had ever been in his life—bone weary.

"OK, well, thanks for your analysis. It's brutal, but not entirely unexpected. I've had the sense for a while that there was going to be a quarter of reckoning—the moment when no one could deny any longer that our problems are not temporary and cyclical, but structural. I get it. But my question for you is: what do we do about it?"

Ted's eyes shifted away from Bob's. "You're not going to like what I have to say."

"That's probably true. But go ahead."

Looking like a prisoner trudging down death row, Ted opened and closed his mouth.

"We have to have layoffs. Massive layoffs. I know that's something that is not in this company's culture. We've never fired anyone except for performance reasons. But, by far, our biggest expense is compensation. We have to cut at a rate faster than we are losing money, and we are losing money at a breathtaking rate."

Bob attempted to project the demeanor of a steely-eyed executive, though he felt like his heart had dropped into his stomach. He took a deep breath and focused on the image of his hands on the desk in front of him.

"I know this, Ted. We have to have layoffs. What I need from you is a point of view about the scope of those layoffs."

A BRUTAL CONFRONTATION

Ted's answer to Bob's question had been unfathomable to the CEO—a reduction of nearly half of the company's work force. Bob had been strongly in favor of layoffs, but he knew that this was a game-changer that would alter the company's culture forever.

Sensing the need to act quickly and decisively, Bob immediately convened a meeting in his office with Ted and Michael. He knew what he had to do. He also knew that—as much as he hated it—his father had to buy in, or at least agree not to start a civil war.

When Ted laid out his proposal, Michael's face turned a fiery red.

"You . . . you," he sputtered. "After all these years, Ted, you turn against me like this? You let my son influence you to such a degree that you are going to lay off more than a hundred good, hard-working, loyal, dedicated employees with families to feed and mortgages to pay?"

"Michael—" Ted said, a pained expression on his face.

"Be quiet, Ted! You have embarrassed me. You have embarrassed yourself. We will not do this, as long as there is breath in my body! People matter. Our people matter.

"But, I'll tell you what—there IS one layoff we need to contemplate."

Michael wheeled to face his son, the CEO, and extended an index finger.

"His!"

THE AFTERMATH

Bob had never been more humiliated in his life. Long after his father had stormed out of his office and Ted had stolen out with a sympathetic glance, Bob remained immobile in his chair.

He considered his options: storm into his father's office and tell him to pack his desk, ignore the confrontation, or maybe start cocktail hour about eight hours early.

Or quit.

There was no way he could work in this environment. No way he could tolerate his father's control. No way he could continue to ignore the fact that though the old man had had a good run—in his day—he was no longer competent enough to manage a business in a rapidly changing and globalizing economy. His father didn't have what it took. But he did have something—control and influence.

Bob's heart rate went up, and his breathing grew ragged. That was the only solution. Quit. He was smart and competent. He was not dependent on his father's largesse or working in a family business. The thing to do was to walk out right now, tell his father where to stick it, and see how Michael would do running the business in such perilous times. That would show him!

Bob heaved himself out of his chair and began to pace, trying to somehow regulate his breathing.

He knew what he needed to do, but he was also overwhelmed by the magnitude of the decision. Leave the family business he had worked so long to lead? Leave the truly good employees to the whims of his controlling and newly incompetent father?

He realized he needed perspective, a deep breath.

He needed to call David.

A TUMULTUOUS CONVERSATION

Half an hour later, David and Bob were seated on the leather chairs in Bob's home office as Bob related the events of the morning.

"Well, first thing," said David, "I'm sorry, Bob. I can't imagine how difficult that conversation must have been for you, how unnerving."

"More than unnerving, David. It was humiliating. He talked to me like I was a boy—like I was totally incompetent. And, you know, he has done that my whole life. Talked down to me, made me feel like I wasn't good enough, tried to control everything. You have no idea what it was like growing up with Michael as a dad."

Bob's face turned red. "Oh, man, that was embarrassing. A grown man talking like he's a little boy." Bob stopped, closed his eyes, and forced his hands to unclench. "Sorry, David. Let's keep the focus on the business issues, OK?"

David said nothing, just smiled gently and nodded slightly.

"So the deal is that my dad had a good run building the business. But those were radically different times. He has no idea how to build the business—rescue the business—today. He's floundering, lost. And the infuriating thing is that the more lost he is, the more control he has to exert. Which is why the only solution is for me to resign. This is absolutely untenable."

After a pause of a few moments, David spoke.

"Bob, let me ask you something. Have you ever met your father before?"

"Um, what? What kind of question is that? I've sort of known him my whole life!"

David smiled. "I didn't mean, have you met Michael before. I meant, have you ever met someone like him, someone who has habits and traits that so annoy you? Specifically, have you ever met someone who combines incompetence and controlling behavior?"

"I don't know exactly what you're asking, but you just put your finger on the two traits that drive me nuts: someone who is controlling while having no idea what to do. Control freaks and incompetent people make me crazy. I avoid them at all costs."

David nodded. "I know. That's not hard to see, Bob. And now, we're getting somewhere. Do you mind if I use your whiteboard again?"

Without waiting for an answer, David rose from his seat, grabbed a green marker, and wrote these words on the board.

We meet the same person over and over again.

"Bob, all of us—not just you—have a list of traits that drive us to distraction. For you, it is the combination of controlling and incompetent. For others, it is a foul mouth or a superior attitude or laziness. These traits elicit powerful emotions within us.

"The real issue, though, is that the traits that have the most power for us are the ones that reside within us, or that we fear reside within us. We don't like to think of those traits as being within us, because we can't stand them. So we don't see them lying within. Is this making sense?"

"I think so," Bob replied. "You're saying that all of us have a list of traits that annoy us and lead us to react negatively toward or avoid those people who demonstrate them?"

"That's right, as far as it goes. But there is more, Bob. A moment ago, I said that we keep meeting the same person over and over—the person who possesses those traits which we despise. You get that. Now let me finish the thought."

On the whiteboard, David wrote a second sentence underneath the first.

And you are that person.

Bob started, sputtering. "David, you had me, but now you have lost me. What do you mean, we are the person who annoys us the most?"

"Good question, Bob. All of us have a part of us that we readily embrace. This is the side of us that we are aware of—the stuff we generally like. Our cheerful, generous, hopeful, encouraging, influential side. But there is another side as well—our unaware side. These are less attractive qualities. And we don't like that we have them, or might have them. So what we tend to do is to push those parts of ourselves away, often even denying that they exist. But the problem is that you can't for long deny a part of yourself. And when we do, self-destructive things start to happen.

"It is a painful thing when we discover that a trait that we despise is really a part of who we are. It hurts, and everything in us wants to deny it. But it is also a gift, because that realization can be the portal to our learning more about who we really are, as opposed to who we think we are."

Bob was beyond puzzled and a little agitated, and David sensed this.

"Bob, I know this has been an incredibly challenging day for you, but I want to pull a few strands of our conversation together. Can we take a few more minutes?"

Bob slowly nodded his head, so David continued.

"When we react so strongly against traits in other people, what we are really doing is reacting to something that is in our own unaware side. Those traits remind us of something that actually exists inside of us, or that we fear might be there. But if we aren't willing to acknowledge that part of ourselves, then there is inner tension and anxiety that grips us. And we have to do something with that anxiety. So we focus it on other people, projecting our own unaware side onto them.

"And here's the thing, Bob. You are doing this with Michael. Michael is like a movie screen to you. You think you are seeing incompetence and controlling tendencies in him—and they may or may not be there. But that's not the point. The fact that you react so strongly to those traits you believe you see in Michael is positive proof that they are actually in you."

Bob felt his cheeks flush and a strange restless energy inside. He shifted uncomfortably in his seat.

"Bob, you have not yet acknowledged your unaware side, your own capacity to be and to do what you see in Michael. He represents the part of you that you fear the most. When you react with anger towards your father, you are really expressing anger at yourself."

Bob clenched his fists. He couldn't help himself. He felt a mounting rage, a not-unfamiliar emotion for him of late. He wanted David to finish and to leave. He wanted to be alone with his thoughts. No, check that. He wanted to be alone so he could sleep. He felt so exhausted.

But David was not quite done.

"There's an old mantra of mine, Bob. And it's going to be the last thing I write on the whiteboard today before I leave you alone."

David grabbed the green marker again and penned these words:

Resistance is your ally.

"Resistance is your ally, not your enemy, because it shows you that your present course of action is not working. I mean both professionally and personally. The business is struggling, and you are miserable. The upshot is that your father is not your enemy. In fact, he can be your very best teacher. What he can show you is that, whether or not he is incompetent and controlling, you are incompetent and controlling—or at least you fear you are. I know that's hard to hear, but—"

"Hard to hear?" Bob exploded. "You're kidding me, right? No, of course not! It's not hard to hear that I am incompetent and controlling. If I am so incompetent and controlling, why did you decide to advise me?"

Bob felt a vein in his temple throbbing, the cords in his neck tightening.

"You've got it all wrong, David. My dad is the controlling, incompetent one. And I am the only one, apparently, who can see it. The problem is, I have no idea what to do about it. And I know that I am the one who has to figure out what to do about it; only I can do that. I thought you would help me with that, and yet you are insulting me in my own house. This meeting is over, done. You know the way out."

David got to his feet slowly. "I got it, Bob. I'm out of here. But one last thing. The fact that you let me say as much as I did shows me that you are beginning to get to some deeper truths about yourself and about life and work. You've put your toe in the water, and that takes courage. I want to encourage you to go all the way and plunge into the deep water. It's worth it. And I won't bug you, but if you want to talk more about it, you know where to find me. Goodnight."

Bob didn't say a word, but rather fixed David with his best hard-ass-CEO glare.

When he heard his front door close, Bob collapsed into his armchair. "Plunge into the deep water, huh?" he sighed wearily. "I'm already in over my head."

CHAPTER FIVE

A STEP TOWARD CHANGE

The next day started poorly. Bob woke up with a splitting headache after a restless night of sleep. Cursing at his alarm clock, he grabbed his iPhone to check on emails that had arrived during the night.

An email from the chairman of the company's board of directors was red-flagged at the top of the list. "Bob, it has come to my attention that we are facing down some major strategic issues. I am convening an emergency board meeting Wednesday night. Please come prepared to talk about your plans to respond to our poor quarterly report, and please don't make any significant decisions until then."

Bob knew exactly what had happened. Ever the masterful tactician, Michael had alerted the chairman to Bob's plans for massive layoffs and had determined to head him off at the pass. Bob saw that the rules of engagement had changed. Now, quitting might not be an option. He was likely to be terminated.

He wasn't sure if he was furious or relieved. The one thing he knew was that he was tired.

He didn't want to go into the office, didn't want to walk past employees he might have to lay off or who might see *him* laid off.

Bob wasn't sure where to turn. He didn't want to be alone—his divorce had confirmed how much he hated being alone. So he called the only person he sensed he could trust, in spite of the conflict of yesterday: David.

A CHANGE OF VENUE

When David answered, he said he was glad to meet with Bob. But he suggested a walk instead of a meeting in a restaurant or in Bob's home. "I think the fresh air would do us both good."

It was brisk outside, a typical late fall Massachusetts day, gray and bracing. The two men walked on a public greenway, almost entirely alone.

Bob told David about his restless night and the board chair's email.

"That's brutal, Bob. What are you going to do?"

Bob sighed deeply, stopped walking, and sank onto a nearby park bench.

"David, I have absolutely no idea. And I'm not sure it matters. The one thing I've always had going for me was self-assurance. Now I'm starting to think I don't have what it takes. I am not going to say this to the board, much less my dad, but I wonder if I'm up to this."

"Bob, I think you need to take the day off, go home, and sleep. I know that's hard for you to hear, but it is what your body and soul need the most. But before you do that, can I offer a couple of reflections to you?"

Bob laughed. "Yeah, sure. You pissed me off yesterday, but to tell you the truth, I am at the limits of my resources. I am willing to try almost anything at this point."

David sat on the bench beside Bob and squeezed the younger man's shoulder for a moment.

"Bob, you have no idea how great it is to hear you say those words. I talked about you going from dipping your toe into the water to plunging into the deep waters, and you sound like a man who may be willing to try."

THE STORY IN EVERY LIFE

"Bob, here's the deal. All of us are telling a story with our lives. It may be a good story, a bad story, or a mediocre story. But every life is a story. And every story has a script. Most of us were given our scripts at a fairly young age, and we spend our lives either living them out or writing our own unique script.

"So we are living out this story, and then the story starts to contain expectations—in your case, expectations that you would take over your dad's company and enjoy smashing success. But the problem is that those expectations collided with your script."

Bob held up his hand. "Script? Story? Look, David, I appreciate your trying to help but, personally, I don't speak the language of Hollywood. I live in a world of balance sheets, P&Ls, and hard-nosed decisions with very little margin for error. You're going to have to help me relate here."

Undeterred, David pressed on. "Your personal script says that you don't measure up. That you might not have what it takes. That you might do 'fine,' but you will never be as successful as Michael. And that script—which you hate, but which you are living into—collided with the expectation that you are supposed to take the company from strength to strength. I can only imagine the pain and anxiety this has created within you, Bob.

"There is a part of you that believes the script that says you don't have what it takes. It says that if people knew you, they would know you were a fraud who is only in the position he's in because he's his father's son. This message about incompetence is a message that far too many people get in our culture, and we internalize it at an early age. I believe you have done that."

Bob felt dizzy. Everything in him wanted to swat away what David was saying, but he stayed mute.

"Bob, I want you to consider the possibility that Michael represents that core message for you: that you are not adequate, that you don't have what it takes, that you are a fraud. You have excellent prowess as an interpreter of balance sheets and profit and loss statements, but all of that pales in comparison to what you really believe deep down: that you are a fraud."

Bob finally spoke, in a subdued voice. "OK, David, I am willing to go with that for a moment. But what does it mean? What do I do with that?"

"That's a great question, Bob. Here's what it looks like. It's a change of strategy. Right now you are transferring your fears and anxieties and inadequacies to Michael because that's safer than facing them in yourself. The new strategy is acknowledging these things in yourself and holding them up to the light where they can be seen for what they are."

Bob thought for a moment and then responded. "David, you said that my dad could be the best teacher I ever had. I know I Red-Zoned over that idea, as you would probably say, but I have been stewing on it. What did you mean?"

CHANGE BEGINS

David leaned back on the park bench, laced his hands behind his head, and smiled broadly.

"Bob, I think we just hit a turning point. You are in the crucible now and are facing it. Things often have to get worse before they can get better, and I think you may have hit that point, even with a difficult board meeting coming up. Bob, remember what I referred to as a mantra of mine?"

"Yeah. 'Resistance is your ally,' right?"

"Right. Here's how you can leverage that concept. Michael can be a great teacher for you because he exposes your fears and brings out stuff in you that is really, really there.

"Now when our real self gets exposed, we can go one of three ways: One, we can deny it and push it aside, which you have done to a degree. I mean, we all do that to a degree. Two, you can push back and punch back, which you have been doing some as it relates to Michael. Or, three, you can do what I believe you now have a real shot at doing—you can pause and reflect on why what you are doing is not paying off. And then, having been taught, you can change your approach to something that will work."

A NON-ANXIOUS PRESENCE

"I know things aren't working," Bob said. "But what exactly am I doing to cause that?"

David paused thoughtfully.

"It's like this, I think. You are trying to compensate for your own doubts about your ability to follow your dad's success and navigate this company through perilous times by working harder and exerting more control. You feel that you desperately have to succeed to demonstrate your competence and that the only way to do this is to be, and to be seen as, the man in charge. Michael's very presence is a sort of threat to both your competence and your sense of control and influence—which might be why you respond so strongly to what you see as his growing incompetence and controlling ways."

David leaned back in his chair, studying Bob's expression. "But remember this, Bob. Michael is not really your problem. He is incredibly anxious these days. He is wondering if his legacy is crumbling and if the employees that he really, deeply cares about will have jobs. But the most anxious person in an organization is always a symbol of the organization as a whole. You can be sure there is anxiety all throughout the company, from the executive offices to the factory floor." Bob nodded, recognizing the connection. David continued.

"The question is whether you, as a leader, are going to contribute to that anxiety or are going to be a non-anxious presence who lowers the anxiety of others and gives the company a shot at succeeding." Bob's gaze turned to the ground and his brow furrowed. David placed a hand on his shoulder, causing Bob to look back up. "Hey, let's walk a little more."

The two men rose from the bench and walked in silence along the tree-lined lane for a time before Bob voiced his thoughts.

"You used an interesting phrase—a 'non-anxious presence.' What exactly is that?"

"When a group is anxious," David started, "what they need more than anything else is for their anxiety to be recognized and understood and brought out into the open. But anxiety has a tendency to spread like a destructive wildfire.

What the group needs is for a leader who is managing his or her own anxiety to create what I call a holding environment—a safe place where the anxiety of the group can be acknowledged, but contained. Over time, as the anxiety level is reduced, the very best resources, smarts, and creativity of the people can tackle any challenges the organization is facing.

"That, Bob, may be your fundamental challenge—to be a non-anxious presence when your own anxiety is so high. That is, quite simply, required if you are going to save this company." David stopped the walk. "Check that. Your fundamental challenge is not to save the company, but to save yourself. And believe me, my friend, the two are linked."

CHAPTER SIX

LESSONS IN PRISON

After David and Bob had finished their walk, Bob went for a long drive instead of going straight home, letting his mind wrap around their conversation. Thoughts still clamored in his mind, even as he went through the routine of grabbing the mail from his mailbox, tossing the bills into a basket on the kitchen counter, nibbling on some sharp Vermont cheddar cheese, drinking a glass of red wine, and finally sitting back in his leather recliner. But the routine was turned on its head because the day was only just reaching its peak, and he knew there was work for him at the office.

It felt weird not being in the office, but Bob was convinced that David was right. He needed some space, some rest. But he couldn't sleep—his brain was humming too fast.

He puttered around the empty house for a bit, restless and agitated. And then his cell phone rang. David's number came up on the screen.

"Bob, I have a spur-of-the-moment proposition, and I trust you aren't going into the office today, right?"

"Yeah, David, I'm trying to take your advice. What's up?"

After a short pause, David responded. "Do you want to go to prison?"

A NEW JOURNEY

Two hours later, David and Bob pulled up in David's car to a nondescript parking lot. The green sign at the entrance to the lot was marked "Summit State Prison." Bob had agreed to go to prison, and he wasn't entirely sure why.

On the phone and in the car, David had explained to Bob that once a month he visited inmates in this prison to build relationships, to encourage the men, to pass on hope, and to conduct workshops on conflict resolution.

"There's quite a market for conflict resolution here," David had quipped. "Lack of conflict navigation skills is why most of the guys are here."

Today was David's day to visit the prison, and since he knew Bob had nothing else planned, David thought to invite him along. Restless, bored, and slightly depressed, Bob had agreed.

They walked into a small beige building, as institutional as was possible to imagine. After climbing the steps to the second floor, they passed through a door with the word

"Warden" printed above a small window. An administrative assistant sat at a small desk inside.

"David!" she said, beaming. "It's so good to see you!"

"Marilyn, you look radiant today! How do you manage it, working for that troll you report to?"

Marilyn laughed, and glanced over her shoulder. "Oh, come on, David. Just because you used to be on the inside, you think you have to pretend to hate the man!"

David threw his head back and laughed. "OK, you got me. I love the dude. Is he in?"

"Yes, I am," said a booming voice, "but why would I have time for the likes of you?"

Bob saw an enormous man coming through the door to the inner office. He was rotund and wore a nicely tailored suit and a big smile.

"Marilyn, you let this miscreant David in here?" the man bellowed. "How could you? Gonna have to go on lockdown now."

The man strode across the office and grabbed David in a bear hug. "On second thought, Marilyn, let's let him stay. At least I can keep an eye on him that way!"

David rolled his eyes. "Bruce, you need some new material. You break out the same routine every month. Bruce Davis, meet Bob O'Reilly. Bob, Bruce."

Bob shook the warden's hand and quickly pulled his own back to check for broken bones.

"Bob, it's good to meet you. David here has told me all about you. Been hearing about you for a lot of years. Can you guys stop in my office for a minute?"

The three men stepped into the warden's office, which was fairly large, but inexpensively furnished: purely functional, early bureaucratic.

The warden snapped his fingers and ducked back out to confer for a moment with his assistant, asking Bob and David to wait. While they waited, Bob fingered a book on the coffee table—*Man's Search for Meaning*, by someone named Viktor Frankl. Bob had never heard of the title.

"Hang around the warden long enough, and you'll hear him talk about that book," said David. As if on cue, the warden ducked back into his office and noticed Bob holding the book.

"Ah, you found my playbook and my Bible for doing this job!"

"I've never heard of the book," Bob replied. "What's it about?"

Bruce waved Bob and David into seats across from his desk.

"Frankl was an eminent psychotherapist early in the twentieth century," the warden began. "Unfortunately, he was Jewish and lived in Germany. He was so brilliant that the Nazis used him for a while to treat others, but eventually he ran afoul of the Third Reich and was put into a concentration camp, along with the rest of his family. His wife and mother died in the camps. Of his family, Frankl was the only one to survive. He founded a school of psychology called logotherapy, but he was best known for writing that book right there on the table. It's the most influential book in my life and career."

Bob was curious. "What makes it so important to you?"

The warden answered quickly, as if he had heard the question before.

"Well, it's a brilliant account of his experiences in the camps, but, even more, it is a testament to the resilience of the human spirit, the ability of mankind to overcome and even triumph in the face of unimaginable pain and loss. Some can accomplish it and others can't, but in this book, Frankl shows a path forward. That comes in handy in my line of work."

Bruce leaned back and took another copy off of his credenza. "But here, don't take my word for it. Read it yourself—a gift from me." He tossed the book across his desk to Bob.

The warden waved aside Bob's thanks. "Now, I know what David is doing here, Mr. O'Reilly, but how about you? What brings you to prison today?"

"I'm honestly not sure. David asked me to come. He's uh—serving as a sort of consultant to me these days, and so I guess I'm interested in seeing part of what makes him tick."

"And I am guessing," Bruce jumped in, "that with his typical modesty, David hasn't told you how important he is around here."

"Now, Warden," David interrupted, but Bruce cut him off with an oversized upraised palm. "Seriously, Bob, you need to understand this.

"David has been able to leverage his own experiences of incarceration to be a transformative influence in the lives of hundreds of men here. He's done a great job as a mentor and coach to many of the men, but the lasting change has been tied to the seminars and workshops he leads on conflict resolution. He's got what I used to think was a crazy idea—that conflict is not only NOT an enemy, but it is actually an ally. As you can imagine, most of the guys who landed in this place did so because they had no idea how to manage conflict.

"I've seen hardened criminals, gang-bangers, and violent and angry men grasp responsibility for the crimes that brought them here; I've seen 'em go from discipline cases to leaders of other men and, in some cases, gain early release and go on to live productive lives. It's remarkable, and even more so because this big lummox of a guy is responsible for it."

The warden burst out into gales of laughter, and David grinned sheepishly.

"Seriously, though, Bob," Bruce continued. "I'm getting you in to see one of these workshops today. You'll be pleasantly surprised.

"Speaking of which," he said, springing to his feet with surprising grace for such a big man. "We need to get you through security and over to the unit if we are going to be on time. Bob, nice to meet you. David, if you guys have time after the workshop, pop your head in a minute. I love seeing your visitors' reactions!"

The three men shook hands, and the warden handed Bob and David off to a corrections officer named Logan. "Gentlemen," said the C.O. "If you will follow me this way."

A LONG WALK

The men made their way through a courtyard and into a low-slung, nondescript building where, after showing their driver's licenses, they took off their shoes, deposited their valuables in gray bins, and went through a metal detector.

Bob assumed they were done, but an officer reached underneath the reception counter and handed them two more things: a visitor name tag and a small plastic whistle, like a child's toy. The man appeared to read Bob's mind as a bemused expression spread across his face.

"This is your recourse if a fight breaks out or if you are threatened in any way. Blow your whistle as loudly and as often as you can, because we'll have to help you in that moment. State law does not allow us to negotiate for the release of hostages in a correctional institution. You'll be on your own if we can't get to you. Gentlemen, have a nice day, now."

Bob gulped and followed David and another officer out the door.

The three men walked through another courtyard laced with high barbed-wire fences. Then they came into the main prison yard surrounded by cell units.

Hundreds of men were out in the open, some doing chin-ups and pull-ups on rudimentary equipment, others playing basketball using a net-less rim, some kicking a soccer ball toward an imaginary goal chalked on a concrete wall.

After a moment, Bob noticed what made the scene seem so weird to him. There were men of every hue and ethnicity in the yard, but they all were clumped with their own kind. There were African-Americans and whites and Latinos; there were Muslims performing their regular prayers on rugs spread out in the yard. But none of the various racial and ethnic groups were interacting in any way.

The February air was chilly, but Bob felt a deeper chill. His concern was not helped by the fact that most of the faces of the men were hard and their eyes were suspicious as he walked past, though he did notice that a few men smiled slightly at David.

After what seemed like an interminable walk, the group arrived at another low-slung building and made for the entrance.

"This is my home-away-from-home here, Bob," David said by way of explanation. "This is a study center where inmates who want to receive treatment for substance abuse or get life skills training can come after they have demon-strated a real desire to change. The conflict-resolution workshop I lead has become the most popular class here. More than 1,200 men have participated!"

The correctional officer led them through the door and into a modest office around the corner before taking his leave of them. There, Bob and David were greeted by a man who introduced himself as Chaplain Fred. He and David hugged, and Fred shook Bob's hand.

"Bob, you heard all of the nice things the warden said about me. This man, Fred, is the real hero in this place!

In the middle of budget cuts and dwindling resources, he keeps providing a source of hope and healing for these men. I don't know how he does it."

"Sit down, guys," said the chaplain, motioning them to worn, utilitarian chairs. There was barely enough room for all three in the small quarters.

"David, I hope you have better luck here today than last time. Bob, I don't know if David told you, but last time there was a note slipped between Latino gangs threatening violence. We had to put the whole place on lockdown. And that meant that David was stuck here with me till ten o'clock at night. No one could leave their building, and the snack machine here doesn't even work." Fred smiled ruefully.

Bob glanced at his toy whistle and tried to maintain a dignified expression.

"But, Bob," the chaplain continued, "I gotta tell you, this is the one building you want to be in at a time like that. The atmosphere in this place is night-and-day different from the rest of the—pardon the expression—joint. You'll see why in a minute."

Seeking to make conversation, Bob asked the chaplain a question. "Fred, I'm sure this is tough work. What led you to do it?"

Fred ran a hand over his close-cut. "Well, I ask myself that question some days, believe me. I used to pastor a small church outside. No great shakes, but it provided a comfort-able-enough living, and I liked the people. But then I started making some weekend visits here, and I realized that you can make a real difference in these people's lives. Not all of them; some choose to sit on their bunks all day, watch TV, and make trouble. But the guys that come in this building— well, some of them make it. Even some of the lifers, the guys that are never getting out of here, embrace the program and become different men."

Interested, Bob leaned forward in his chair. "What makes the difference for them?" he asked.

The chaplain answered quickly. "Really, just one thing. They decide that their life is not over because they are incarcerated. The ones who believe their life is over are the ones who give up hope and become problems for us in here. The ones who do make it realize that their life is different, but that doesn't mean it has to be without hope or meaning. Right, David?"

David nodded enthusiastically. "Dead right. By the way, the warden gave my friend here a copy of the Frankl book. What Fred is saying, Bob, could be Frankl speaking himself.

"Frankl made the keen observation that the men who ran the Nazi concentration camps could take almost everything from a person. He experienced it firsthand. They could take away freedom, dignity, the lives of one's loved ones, physical health, a vocation, the ability to speak and associate freely, even life itself. But there was one thing they couldn't take away."

Really engaged now, Bob leaned forward again. "And what's that?"

The chaplain interrupted David before he could answer. "You know, David, I have an idea. Let's see if, after the workshop, Bob can come up with the answer to his own question."

"I love it!" David laughed. "And, now, isn't it about time to get started?"

A LIFE-CHANGING FORTY-FIVE MINUTES

A few minutes later, David and Bob entered a classroom where workshop participants, dressed in orange prison-issue shirts, began to file in. Bob noticed that some wore blue jeans while others wore prison-issue pants. He asked David about it and learned that the men in jeans had friends or family on the outside that took care of some of their needs. The men in orange pants had mostly been renounced by their families. Bob imagined that some of these inmates had put their families through hell on earth, but he still felt a stab of sympathy for those who had no one on the outside.

As more men came into the room, Bob watched their eyes light up as they saw David, many of them giving their mentor a fist bump or a hug. Bob noticed two other things as well. First, the room was filled with about thirty men who were a cross-section of those in the prison yard: white, African-American, Latino. But these men were together in the same room. And, second, many of them were giving each other fist bumps and hugs as well. What a contrast! What could explain the difference between the classroom and the prison yard?

After a few minutes, David indicated that they were ready to begin, and the men took seats against the four walls of the room. Bob noticed that they all had well-worn, dog-eared copies of the workshop manual David had prepared. Some had Bibles as well; one had a Koran.

David introduced Bob, and the latter was surprised by the warm greetings the men called out. "Glad you're here, bro!" "Thanks for coming and hanging with us!" "Any friend of Dave's is a friend of ours!"

David asked one of the men to read the portion of the manual they were to study tonight, and as the next few minutes unfolded, Bob received one of the greatest shocks of his life.

NOT SO CONCRETE

On the car ride to the prison, David had mentioned that today's objective was to review and hit the highlights of the concept of Red Zone/Blue Zone, the concept Bob had learned just a few days earlier. Bob had immediately puzzled at that. Red Zone/Blue Zone, he thought, was a pretty heady concept. He wasn't sure he fully grasped it himself. He assumed—accurately, as it would turn out—that many of the inmates had limited educational backgrounds. Bob assumed that their minds would work concretely and that Red Zone/Blue Zone might be over their heads.

Boy, was he wrong.

As the men began to discuss the concepts of the night, Bob was blown away by the level of sophistication, detail, and nuance in their understanding. From their underlined copies of the manual, it was clear that they had spent hours thinking about, digesting, and, most importantly, internalizing the material. Bob found himself wishing he could take notes to aid his own understanding.

One man, Terence, said, "I see now that, in my family, I was only ever taught to Red-Zone. So that's all I knew. To tell you the truth, when I first learned about the Zones, man, I was angry. I felt cheated, like I had never been given a fair chance in life. And then I realized that I can apply the principles right here, right now. I don't have to wait, and I don't have to live with regrets. I can live a good, Blue-Zone life now."

An older, soft-spoken, bespectacled man named James had this to say: "I am fifty-three years old, and I have been here since I was twenty-one. I have a parole hearing in a couple months, and the lawyer actually thinks I have a shot at getting out this time. But sometimes, I worry. Have I learned this stuff deeply enough? The first time someone crosses me, will I have gone deep enough in the Blue Zone that I can respond that way?"

The men paused for a few moments to give verbal encouragement to James, and the chaplain, who had poked his head in the room to say hello, added: "I am going to be a lifeline for you, my brother. Anytime you need me on the outside, all you have to do is call." The room erupted in cheering, clapping, and whistling.

The youngest man in the room, body full of gang tattoos, looked wistful. "If I had known about the Blue Zone, man, I would never have banged, never have done those things I did that got me here." The room was silent and respectful. The young man would have many years to absorb that lesson.

All too soon for Bob's taste, David was drawing the meeting to a close and thanking the men. On the way out, every man in the room, shook Bob's hand and thanked him for coming. Soon, an officer came to lead David and Bob back out into the chilly afternoon, back through the prison yard.

As they walked, David asked, "Well, what did you think?"

Bob thought for more than a minute. "I think the men grasped your material, and I think they love you. Also, the contrast between the yard and the classroom is blowing me away. Such a total lack of tensions between different races and religions."

David nodded. "That's the main reason we have such strong support from the warden and from most of the officers in leadership. Their biggest day-to-day problem is violence between gangs and different races. They aren't even allowed to sit together in the mess hall. At any given moment, an insult, a slur, even a look can incite a race war and people—officers—can get hurt. Our program is literally the only place in this prison where those tensions are being reduced. It's one of the things that keeps me coming back here. It's so satisfying."

The men were silent for the rest of the walk back to the reception area as they handed back their name tags and whistles and collected their personal belongings.

Quickly, they ducked into the main administration building to see if the warden was still there. He was, but he only had a moment. "Hey, David, the chaplain called over here while you were in your session. He said our friend Bob had asked a great question, and he was wondering if he had discovered the answer. So?"

David smiled. "That is our afternoon conversation in the car ride home, my friend. We'll get out of your hair. See you next week." Bob appreciated being let off the hook and gratefully shook hands with the warden and left.

A PROBING QUESTION

As the men buckled their seatbelts to begin the journey home, Bob was preemptive.

"Short answer, David: I don't have the answer to your question about Frankl. It sounds to me as if the Nazi guards could and did take everything away from him. I can't imagine what was left. He lost freedom, health, his loved ones, every-thing but his own life, but you said one's own life was not the answer. I'm stumped."

"That's OK, Bob, it's a hard question. Here is what Frankl said, in essence. Every freedom a person has can be taken away but the freedom to choose how they respond in a given situation. That is the one dignity that can never be denied. And it is an inestimably great power. It means that none of us are victims and none of us are ever far from a fresh, new start in our lives. In the terms of the workshop discussion, it means that, no matter what happens, we can always choose to live in the Blue Zone. And we'll be better leaders, better managers, and better people as a result." David glanced over at Bob in the passenger seat.

"Here is how I see that applying to you in this very hard time for you, Bob: Michael convened a board meeting in a way that feels undermining to you. In fact, the board may be conspiring against you. They may be able to hamstring you, thwart your efforts to lead, and back forces you believe are opposing you. They may even be able to take away your position and compromise your legacy at the company you have given your adult life to help build. But they cannot take away your freedom to choose how *you* respond." Then he paused, waiting for Bob to look at him. "And that, Bob, is why I wanted you to go to prison."

CHAPTER SEVEN

STYLES IN LEADERSHIP

I t had been a life-changing day, and that evening, Bob found it difficult to relax. He tried going for a walk, but turned back after less than half a mile. He tried flipping channels, but couldn't concentrate on either a comedy or a reality show. Finally, he grabbed a rocks glass, an ice bucket, and a tumbler of Evan Williams bourbon, moved into his library, settled into his favorite chair, and sighed.

As he swirled the amber liquid in his glass, he replayed the events of the day. It was clear that many of the incarcerated men had a sense of inner peace and tranquility that eluded him. His life was one adrenaline rush, one business struggle, one nurtured resentment after another. He had affluence, good friends, and—until recently—business success, yet he wasn't happy. These men had lost their freedom and, in many cases, their families, and many had burdened consciences, but they displayed a zest for life and a real hope for the future.

I wonder who the one in prison actually is? he mused.

He took a deep sip of his whiskey and felt it warm his throat and stomach. But he didn't want to rely on alcohol to be his source of solace this evening. He sensed that something bigger was afoot, some coming change that he was either going to have to embrace or deny. Either way, Bob knew he had to make a choice about the path ahead, personally and professionally.

THINGS COME INTO SHAPE

Bob and David had agreed to meet the next day at Bob's house. David had said he needed a whiteboard again, and Bob wondered what his new friend was going to draw this time. The Red Zone/Blue Zone diagrams had paid off handsomely, and Bob was eager to see what was next.

Once Bob was seated, David moved to the whiteboard and drew a simple triangle.

"It's not geometry class, no matter what it looks like, Bob," David said, smiling. "I want to introduce you to a new concept this morning that I think will go a long way toward helping you navigate your current business dilemma. Think of the Red Zone and the Blue Zone as helping you position yourself personally to handle conflict. And think of this concept which I am about to introduce as helping you position yourself professionally to handle the wide variety of challenges a business leader faces.

"Here's the basic premise: leadership is all about identifying and overcoming challenges. But not all challenges are the same. Broadly speaking, there are three main types of challenges we will face. Let's call the first type tactical challenges."

David wrote the word "Tactical" over the left side of the triangle.

"These are the most common types of problems. Think of them this way. When it snows and your driveway is covered, your challenge is getting dug out so you can get to work. You don't need to hire a consultant or convene a think tank. You just need to grab a shovel and dig in or hire the kid down the street to do it. The problem is one that can be solved by using specialized knowledge you already have or finding the right expert who has the solution."

Bob nodded. "That makes sense to me. When we have an IT problem at the office, we bring our tech guys in, or if it's over their head, we hire an IT consultant. Typical business problems. Got it."

David agreed. "Yes, but there is a catch here. A lot of leaders imagine that every problem is this type of problem, and so they believe that all they need to do is to hire the right expert. But many problems are more complex than that. Before we get too far down the trail, let me frame it this way. Each side of the triangle—I call this the 'Leadership Triangle,' by the way—represents a specific sort of leadership challenge. The challenge of a leader is to identify which type of challenge is in front of him or her at any given moment. Knowing what kind of challenge you are facing opens up a range of options from which a leader can choose a response.

"Each type of challenge has several components in terms of the right response: the leader's role, the leader's tone, the questions the leader must ask and get the group to ask, the style of relating the leader chooses, the way the leader approaches the problem, and the tense the leader must live in."

David went back to the board, drew four columns, and put the following information on the chart:

	TACTICAL	STRATEGIC	TRANSFORMATIONAL
ROLE	Expert	Synthesizer	Facilitator
TONE	Confident	Vision casting	Creative
KEY QUESTION	What's wrong?	What's the focus?	What's the Question?
PROBLEMS ARE TO BE . . .	Solved	Planned	Reframed
INTERACTION	Training	Inspiring	Free-flowing and Robust
TENSE	Present	Future	Past, Present, and Future

"For the tactical option, the role of the leader is to be the expert or the expert-finder. Not much need to mess around; just solve the problem. The tone of the leader is confident—'we have the base of knowledge we need to solve this problem right away.'

"The tactical leader's question is simple: 'What's wrong here?' The goal is to uncover, then fix, the evident problems. The leader's style of relating is that of a trainer, bringing current knowledge and wisdom to bear on the present problem. The way the leader approaches the problem is simply to solve it. And, finally, the tense the leader must live in is the present. Ask, 'How can we solve the problem right away so that our today can be better?' Does all of this make sense so far?"

"Yes," Bob replied. "Pretty basic day-to-day business stuff, right?"

"Right, but be careful. The stakes get higher as we fill in the Triangle."

David turned to the whiteboard and wrote the word "Strategic" next to the right side of the triangle.

"The second category of challenges is strategic ones. These challenges are the result of something changing in the external environment of the organization that requires change and adaptation. This is the mom-and-pop store on the corner suddenly having to compete with the low-cost, behemoth chain that moves in on the opposite corner, or the brick-and-mortar bookstore being forced to contend with a growing market for e-readers."

"I get that kind, too," Bob interjected. "It's the reality we face that our competitors are moving manufacturing to countries with lower labor costs and that they are willing to slash their workforce when we have to deal with a no-lay-offs policy." Bob stood and walked closer to the whiteboard, feeling like this was finally something that pertained directly to his company problems. The ideas seemed to ignite within him, burning with excitement.

"Exactly. Stickier problems than the tactical kind." David began to fill in the second row on the chart he had drawn.

"When the challenge is strategic, the leader's role is that of a synthesizer, bringing together knowledge and information from throughout the organization and even calling on outside sources of knowledge. The leader's tone is one of casting vision; you lead with the attitude that 'we can confront this changing environment and continue to be a winning organization.'

"The key question in facing strategic challenges is, 'What should be our focus?' The answer is about where the organization needs to marshal its energies to move ahead. The leader's way of relating to followers is inspirational, rallying them to a bright vision of the future, and the tense is obviously that very same future. The way a leader tackles a strategic challenge is by planning: planning for the problem by always scanning the external environment and planning carefully for how the group is going to tackle the problem in an effective way."

Bob lost a bit of the fire burning in his eyes. "Wow. I think of myself as primarily a strategic leader, and as you are speaking, I see how short I am falling on the inspirational, visionary piece. I have been so immersed in our strategic problems and finding the right solutions that I have not even thought about inspiring my employees."

David looked at him kindly. "You're not the first leader to do that, believe me. But this is why understanding the Leadership Triangle is so important. You have identified the problem correctly as a strategic one, but you have been using a tactical approach—fixing the problem. The irony is that using the wrong set of leadership options can actually make the problem worse."

Both men were silent for a good while, staring at the triangle and the chart on the whiteboard.

David broke the silence after a time. "We still have one type of challenge to discuss. I think you will see that this part of our discussion will be even more relevant for you than strategic challenges." Bob raised an eyebrow.

Underneath the third side of the Leadership Triangle, David wrote "Adaptive Transformational."

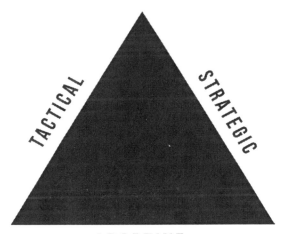

**ADAPTIVE
TRANSFORMATIONAL**

"Transformational challenges. Ah, yes. Bob, this is where the real work of leadership is done, and all too few are willing to go there. Transformational challenges are the ones that engage an organization at the levels of values, beliefs, and behavior. These are where passions collide, emotions run high, and loss is threatened. These are the tough challenges that senior leaders get paid good money to tackle. And the stakes are high, because if an organization puts off or refuses to engage with transformational challenges, then it will eventually wither and die.

"When a leader is facing a transformational challenge, his or her role is that of a facilitator, inviting dialogue and discovery, especially in the arenas of values and beliefs. The tone is one of creativity, inviting and modeling new approaches to problem-solving, even to the extent of provoking conflict! He knows that the key question is 'What *is* the question?' The leader recognizes that before the problems can be solved, they have first to be reframed." David watched Bob's expression change before continuing. Bob returned to his chair, feeling heavy with information.

"The leader's way of relating to the group now has to be open-handed and permission-giving. Everything is on the table. The leader invites a free-flowing and robust dialogue across as many levels of the organization as are affected by the transformational issues. And, finally, all of the tenses are in play here—past, present, and future."

Bob interrupted. "Wait. I want to probe a couple of things with you there. First, what do you mean when you say the key question is 'What's the question?'"

"Good question," David laughed at his pun. "Actually, it is. What I mean is that leaders often fall into the fallacy of believing that their primary job is to come up with answers. In fact, sometimes the right questions lead to deeper answers and offer more profound change. And, for another thing, when the leader spends all of his time in question-answering mode, he actually robs his people of some of their work, which is a subtle form of disrespect."

Bob was startled. "I've never heard anything remotely like that before! I've always thought that leaders were paid more and given more responsibility because they had proven they had the skills and had amassed the experience to have the best answers. You're offering a whole new twist on leadership here." He spread his hands in a *What now?* gesture and sank deeper into his chair.

"Bob, you're right that many followers look to their leaders for all of the answers, but that's only because they have been conditioned to do so. The very best transformative leaders know that their main job is to ask the right questions and frame the right questions so that every ounce of potential, insight, experience, and goodwill is pulled from the group."

Bob thought a moment. "OK, I can see that, provisionally. But I want to hit another thing you said while it is still fresh. I know you have mentioned this reframing thing before, but I don't think I get it in this context. Can you give me an example?"

David responded quickly. "You bet. I heard a great example this past week. A famous artist learned late in life that his father had given up painting when his son was born to take on a second job to provide for the family's needs and to focus on his son. Initially, the son was crushed, feeling

that his own career had been built on the ashes of his father's dream. His burden was relieved only when a friend
said, 'You know, maybe what actually happened was more
like this: your father's passion for art provided the fuel for
your own. His dream actually came to reality in and through
you.' That was a reframe from 'What did I cost my father?'
to 'What did my father give to me?'"

"Wow," was Bob's first response. "I think I see the power
that I could have as a leader."

"I think I want to drive home just a few other concepts
today. The first relates to how the three challenges repre-
sented by the Leadership Triangle interrelate. All tactical
problems are simply tactical. All strategic challenges have
at least some tactical components. And all transformational challenges have some tactical and strategic components.
The level of complexity increases as an issue arrives at the
transformational level.

"So this means that you must think long and hard about
what sort of problem you are actually dealing with. Don't
miss that a challenge is transformational simply because
you can only see its tactical and strategic components.
Drill down deeply, asking questions like 'Are emotions
high here?' 'Are the same failures being repeated?' 'Are we
talking about deeply held values and beliefs?' 'Do we keep
getting the same people in the room in an effort to solve the
problem, yet have the same frustrating results?'

"These are all indications that a transformative challenge
may be on the table." David glanced at the clock.

"Do you have time for one more thing today, Bob?" When Bob nodded, David stepped back to the whiteboard.

"An incredibly important thing to keep in mind as you lead transformative change is that the stakeholders involved in the challenge will be feeling increasing levels of anxiety. You've got to continue to be the non-anxious presence in the process, and one of the best ways of doing this is by asking questions for and about them."

David took up a marker and wrote these questions on the board:

What exactly is their stake in this issue?

What results do they truly desire?

What is their level of engagement in the issue?

What is the degree to which each one holds power and influence, and how are they exercising those things?

What are their core, underlying values?

What are their loyalties and obligations?

What potential losses are at stake for them (status, comfort, identity, time, money, power, control, influence)?

What hidden alliances might they have?

David sat down in his chair for the first time in a while.

"OK, Bob, I know this is like drinking water from a fire hose, but all of that content was leading up to two questions." He paused to let that sink in. "The two most important questions you must ask now are these: As a leader, and as a company, are the challenges I am facing tactical, strategic, or transformational? And what must I do with my answer to that question?"

Bob nodded. "Fair enough, David. I think I have an answer to those questions for my business challenges. But what do you think?"

David smiled. "As much as I would like to weigh in, I am mindful of the fact that a good leader—which I am trying to be—must focus on asking questions, not answering them. I really want to hear your thoughts."

Bob blew out a deep breath, puffing his cheeks.

"OK, then. Well, clearly this is not a tactical issue alone. I mean, a lot of very smart people, most seasoned in this industry with great track records, have been beating their heads against a wall. It's not about finding an expert or drawing on our base of knowledge. So it's not a purely tactical problem. We're at a new place.

"I have been thinking that this is the biggest strategic challenge of my career. So, until the last twenty minutes or so, I would have been rock-solid sure that this was a strategic challenge. And there are huge strategic elements to this. All of this has to do with stuff outside our organization—the shifts in the global economy, the economic slowdown here in the States, our competitors changing the rules of engagement.

"But I see transformational elements as well. The fact that we are clashing over values: old guards versus new guards, a no-layoff policy versus the need to reduce expenses and remake ourselves in a new marketplace." Bob ran his fingers through his hair, buying a moment to gather all his thoughts.

"So given your statement that tactical issues are tactical alone, and strategic issues are tactical plus strategic, and transformational issues involve all three . . . well, given that, I have to say I am facing a transformational challenge and so I better behave as a transformational leader."

David sat back in his chair, showing pleasure in spite of himself. "Yes, you nailed it. So what are you going to do about it?"

The words came out of Bob's mouth even before he had time to process them. "I've got to go talk to my father. I have to bring the insights of Red Zone/Blue Zone together with the actions of a transformational leader."

CHAPTER EIGHT

A TIME OF TRANSFORMATION

B ob woke up the next morning with a level of energy he had not felt in months, perhaps years. After enjoying orange juice, a whole-wheat bagel, and a handful of blueberries, he made coffee. He took his mug to the back deck and sat skimming the newspaper on his tablet, sipping coffee, and enjoying the chill in the air. He felt hopeful, alive.

He finished the paper and scrolled to the document he had written the previous night, summarizing his insights around the Red Zone/Blue Zone concept and the Leadership Triangle. He renewed his resolve to live every moment, to the greatest extent he could, in the Blue Zone. He reminded himself of his commitment to be the best tactical and strategic leader he could be, but to not shy away from—in fact, to seek out—opportunities to be a transformational leader.

This was no mere intellectual exercise. Today was one of the most important meetings of his life, and he would have to be at the very top of his game in exercising his new skills. He was going to meet with his father, Michael.

Bob flipped his tablet cover closed, drained his coffee cup, and looked out over his forested backyard. He breathed deeply, inhaling and exhaling with intentionality. Images of his career at the family company flickered through his consciousness, times of triumph and times of peril and times of failure. After a few minutes, his thoughts centered down into now, this day, this moment.

IT ALL COMES TOGETHER

Bob drove to the office in a relaxed frame of mind, concentrating on his driving. He parked and made his way to his office, taking care to make eye contact with and greet each employee he encountered. Several of them did a double take as Bob walked past. They weren't used to this sort of behavior from him.

He stopped briefly by his office to gather some notes and to deposit his briefcase. Glancing at the mirror on the back of his office door, he straightened his tie. After one more deep breath, he headed down the hall to Michael's office.

His father was waiting for him, eyeing him warily. Their argument last week had left a real strain in their relationship. In Michael's mind, they would always be father and son and their bond could not be broken, but, at this moment, it was frayed. Bob saw this in his father's eyes, and he understood. Just two days ago, he would have felt the same way. As it was, he felt a little nervous about how the conversation was going to go.

Michael nodded at a chair across from his desk. "Sit down, son." After a moment's hesitation, Michael rose from his chair, walked around his desk, and took a seat beside Bob.

Michael cleared his throat. "Bob, I know that the prospect of this board meeting is not an enticing one for you. It's not for me either. But if you've asked to meet today to ask whether or not I was behind it, I can tell you that is not the case. I hated our conversation last week and I do not agree with your proposed direction, but at this point in our respective careers, I am not going to play board politics with you. I will be there as a participant, not a conspirator."

Bob considered his father's words. "I accept that, Dad. I believe you. And I appreciate that. But that's not why I asked to see you today. And, honestly, I didn't really even want our disagreement last week to be the focus of our meeting today."

Bob could see that Michael was both relieved and puzzled.

"It's actually . . . well, the reason I wanted to see you is more because of something going on in me."

Bob paused for a moment to gauge Michael's reaction. It was not common for the two to talk about feelings and inner-goings-on. His father looked interested and perplexed, but not uncomfortable, so Bob continued.

"Dad, you'll be interested, and probably incredulous, to know that David and I have been spending a lot of time together over the last week." Seeing Michael's amazement, Bob hurried to explain. "When I terminated David, he said something that confused me. Actually, two things. He said that I had all the power in this company and he wondered whether, if I got my way in the conflict between you and me over layoffs, I would get what I really wanted." Bob ran his fingers through his hair, smiling.

"This really threw me for a loop, because I assumed that you were still holding onto the reins of power and that if I got my way, I would, by the nature of things, get what I really wanted. But something in David's questions got me thinking. So I asked him to act as a sort of personal consultant to me, and we have met a number of times in the last week."

Bob noticed Michael chuckling. "Oh my, boy-o, that sure sounds like our David. He has a way of making you look at things in a different way—'reframing,' I think he calls it—that makes you wonder for a moment if the sky is up or down. Then he just sort of waits while you figure out which end is up. And, lo and behold, suddenly you see things in an entirely new way. I've experienced this more than once myself."

Bob nodded vigorously. "That's exactly it! But for me, my new way of looking at things had to do with me, not a business problem.

"He explained the concept of the Red Zone and the Blue Zone to me. He explained that resistance is my ally, not my enemy, because it shows me the strategies I have been using aren't working. When I see that, it opens me up to new possibilities. And he showed me that I tend to personalize conflict rather than making the conflict stay within the bounds of business questions and values. That's what happened here in your office last week, and I own my responsibility for that.

"And then he explained that I have been thinking about leadership in all the wrong ways. He showed me that there are three kinds of leadership challenges: the tactical, which are simply about expertise and fixing things; the strategic, which are about changes outside the organization that affect the organization's internal decision-making processes; and, finally, the transformational, which are all about values, beliefs, and behavior. I've been treating every problem as if it were tactical or strategic, never pausing to ask if there was another way." Bob waited for Michael to look him in the eye before continuing, hoping that his father would witness the new zeal and understanding in his expression.

"Dad, the challenges facing us now are a combination of strategic and transformational. But we've got to employ transformational ways of thinking, questioning, relating, and leading if our company is going to survive. Does any of this make sense?"

Michael shifted in his chair. "It does, to a degree. David has mentioned some of this stuff to me before, but I was never one for the soft stuff, you know? Show me a customer to woo or a manufacturing process to fix and I'm all over it.

But David always seemed to have this Zen thing going, as if he knew some sort of secret knowledge. It's beyond me."

Bob laughed. "You know, I thought that at first, too. But when he spells it all out, these concepts make sense. They are simply the way the world works. And I have been so busy for so many years trying to make the world work my way, I never saw it."

Michael cleared his throat, a bit uneasily. "Well . . . I'm glad you are finding out things from David that are helpful for you. As for me, I'm an old dog on the way out the door. But as long as I have the position of senior adviser, I have to ask you this question: how does what you have learned impact what you are going to say to the board and the direction in which you want to take the company?"

"It's a tough question, Dad. But I think there are even more important matters to deal with first. Like our relationship. Yours and mine."

Michael raised his eyebrows. "Look, Bob, we will always be father and son, but right now we have to save this business."

Bob shook his head. "The business is important, sure. But the legacy of the business will be impacted by how we navigate this transition, how well we lead as we try to save this company." Bob took a shaky breath.

"Here's the bottom line. I have spent a lot of years trying to force the world to work on my terms. I had to prove myself to you—to prove myself to me—and it made me a driven man. I got consumed with winning at all costs. And it was a big reason why I lost my marriage. I haven't been happy, Dad. A successful man, but not a happy one.

"The fact is, I lived in the Red Zone, and it has eaten me alive. I'm not going to do that anymore. As we move ahead, whatever the future may hold, I will do my best to lead from the Blue Zone and to never miss a chance to be a transformational leader. It's not about me. It's about our shared values and sense of mission."

Michael O'Reilly sat still for a very long moment, not meeting Bob's gaze. Then he got out of his chair and stood looking out of his office window for a long minute. Still facing the window, Michael finally spoke, his voice gruff.

"What do you need from me, Bob?"

Bob came and stood beside his father and mentor.

"First, I need you to listen to me. You have instilled some great values in this company, values like treating our employees with dignity and respect, honoring customers, always doing the right thing. Our strategy may need to change, but we have to preserve those values. So, I thank you and I promise to do that.

"Second, I need you to be a trusted adviser to me after I become CEO. Heck, I need that now. I have some ideas for a way David can play a role like that, too, but I'm still mulling it over. But as for you and me, that's the way I want us to relate—allies focusing on the business, disagreeing when we have to, but making sure we are having the right kind of disagreements. I need your advice and counsel, Dad."

Michael considered his son's words. Then he turned, looked his son straight in the eye, and grasped Bob's hand firmly. "You have my commitment, son."

AN UNEXPECTED TURN

On Wednesday afternoon, Michael and Bob strode down the corridor to the boardroom. The other members of the board were already there, and both men shook hands all around. Michael's eyes widened ever so slightly when he saw an unexpected presence sitting in one of the chairs ringing the boardroom wall. David. The old friends nodded their greetings.

Soon the chairman of the board called the meeting to order. He gazed coolly around the room and went through the familiar meeting-opening proceedings.

He looked around the room again and spoke of the real purpose of the meeting.

"Gentlemen, we meet today because our last quarterly report was dire. You all know the results, so I won't belabor those painful points. We all know we need to change things significantly. But we must make those changes without violating our company's values, the most important of which is that we take care of our people and do not lay them off.

"As we have been made aware, the CEO-designate voiced his desire that we must have layoffs if the company is to be successful. Many of us cannot even countenance such a thought. So we thought it wise to meet today to hear from Bob himself.

"And," the chairman added pointedly, "to consider alternative leadership scenarios."

The chairman shuffled the papers in front of him and nodded to Bob.

Bob felt his heart rate increase and his skin flush at the implied threat. But he looked down at the legal pad in front of him where he had written "Blue Zone," took an extra breath, and nodded respectfully back to the chairman.

"Thank you, Mr. Chairman. And thank you for the opportunity to explain my thoughts and plans. We all know that our situation is dire. There are some tactical things in our processes we may need to fix. There are certainly many dark clouds on the horizon in terms of our competitors that require strategic shifts. But the most important challenges we face are of a different kind. They are questions of values and beliefs. What kind of company are we going to be? Really, the largest question is whether we're going to have a company worth saving."

Quizzical looks and raised eyebrows came from around the table.

"A week ago, I erred. I made a strong statement and issued several orders that left no room for compromise. In the last week, I have been forced to take a hard look at my leadership style and even my values.

"With a significant change in perspective, I will outline where I think we should go. As the CEO-designate, I don't

have all of the answers. In the present case, I don't even have
a majority of the answers. I can come up with the experts
to solve our tactical challenges. I have a pretty good strategic mind and am comfortable taking the lead there. But I
cannot answer for this company what it wants to be. I can
give leadership to the process of answering that question,
but the answer is not mine alone to give.

"Take our no-layoffs policy, for example. My business
mind sees no way to move forward without layoffs. Yet I
understand how deeply rooted the value of no layoffs is to
our company. I'll respectfully disagree with the chairman
that our no layoffs policy is our most important value. It is
one in a cluster of competing values which must be navi-
gated here.

"One value is no layoffs. Another is the survival of the en-
terprise and maintaining market viability. It seems that we
must choose one or the other. But there must be another
way, and that way will be found in the wisdom of the
group, the people who make up this great company. We
must have robust discussions and conversations around
such topics. So I have two proposals today." Bob held up
his first finger.

"First, I propose that we create a new company officer:
the Chief of Transformational Leadership. This person's
role would be to advise me and this board to ensure that
we are focused on the right values and conversations and
that we are honoring a leadership culture and healthy decision-making processes."

Bob paused a little for dramatic effect, now holding up two fingers.

"And I propose that this person be David Thomas." Bob gestured to his friend and heard the gasps of surprise from around the room.

"I know that I terminated David last week and word has gotten around as to the part of his past that led me to that decision. But I have come to believe it was a rash and unwise decision. I spent a lot of time with David and visited with him as he volunteered at a prison nearby. I have seen that he is a person of unconquerable courage and integrity, possessed of unusual wisdom. He is the perfect man for this role, and this time.

"I propose that David lead the way in engaging conversations around the transformational issues we are facing so that we will have the best, richest information by which to make wise decisions." Bob lowered his hand to his side and looked around the table, meeting each gaze.

"But, friends, I would like to share with you the most important thing I have learned. I see now that the greatest weakness of my entire professional life is that I have viewed conflict as my enemy, something to be feared and fought.

"As a result, I have avoided tough issues or simply run over people in an effort to avoid dealing with competing values." He paused for a moment and looked around, almost as if he were seeing a new room.

"I have to tell you, this has had severe consequences in both my personal and professional life. What I have come to understand is that conflict—healthy conflict—is not something to be avoided, but rather something to be embraced.

"It's not too much to say that conflict can be an ally, even a friend. Moving forward, I hope and trust this company will be characterized by vigorous debate and even conflict around values. We'll all be better for that because healthy conflict shows us that our current strategies are not working and gives us a path forward with more options than we had before.

"Ladies and gentlemen of the board, as a leader, I need you. I need your counsel. I need to trust you. And you need to trust me. I am absolutely convinced that within this company lies everything we need to navigate these choppy waters and return to our position as a market leader. Our best days lie ahead."

And he was done.

There was nothing but silence for a while. Then a few members asked questions, several indicated enthusiasm, one or two muttered about "getting on with it" and "radical ideas." Finally, the chairman summed up.

"The fact is that both proposals are under the purview of the CEO, and that person is still Michael." All eyes in the room turned to the elder O'Reilly.

"I figured we were coming to that," Michael said. "I'll keep it simple. These proposals, and Bob as my successor, have my unqualified support. I only wish I had instigated them long ago."

And that was that. The meeting adjourned, and the members filed out, several of them quietly congratulating

David, one of them whispering in Bob's ear, "I don't envy your position."

Finally, only David, Bob, and Michael were left.

Michael spoke first. "Well, I'm surprised by all this, David. Surprised and delighted. Welcome back! Only this time we'll get you a nice office up on this floor."

David shook his head. "Oh, no you don't," he protested. "I won't have time to be in an office. I'll have to be out on the front lines all day, every day. Beginning right now."

His adrenaline beginning to wear off, Bob was muted. "I feel great about this direction, but I don't know if it will work. I don't know if we can navigate competing values in a way that leaves the company intact. There are a lot of unknowns out there. I'm all in, but I am also not naïve."

David nodded. "I don't disagree with anything you just said, Bob, but I do know one thing for sure. You are a different leader and a different man now. You have started your voyage toward becoming a transformational leader. You can meet conflict and see its purpose in strengthening you and the firm. And no matter what happens, that can only be taken away from you if you allow it to be."

The three men shook hands, exchanged determined looks, and walked to their offices on the executive level and on the factory floor.

PART TWO

L ife can be dangerous. As people negotiate life's waters, most would implicate conflict as the top culprit that makes life such a challenge—conflict in marriage, in employment, in communities, in governments, and between nations.

Much of living is also about leadership, and leadership is about conflict. "Oh," you might say, "I'm not a leader." But we would argue that you are—in your families, in your friendships, in your neighborhoods, in any of your close associations. Leadership is not so much about formal roles about activities where we must stand up and take responsibility.

Others of you who are reading this book are in formal positions of leadership. You undoubtedly face conflict challenges daily, in one form or another. Because we coach many leaders across the organizational spectrum, we know that a significant amount of a leader's time is caught up in conflict. But that's not all bad; at least, it doesn't have to be all bad. The healthiest organizations are loaded with conflict, as are the least healthy. It's not the conflict, per se, that determines an organization's health; it's the very nature of that conflict that counts.

CHAPTER NINE

CONFLICT: FRIEND OR FOE?

Most people run from conflict. And yet, conflict has a niggling habit of continually showing up, even though every possible measure is taken to prevent it. We have a different slant on conflict:

- You can't escape conflict. The issues on which we can disagree are endless.
- Conflict isn't really the problem. Conflict is not only *not* a bad thing, it's a good thing, and a necessary thing. The problem is how people relate to one another when they are in conflict.

The purpose of this appendix is to guide readers through three simple principles that are indispensable to be successful in life.

The process demonstrated in this appendix will be a great starting point for transforming your outlook on yourself and on conflict. It is designed to provide you with the tools you need to bring about transformation.

GETTING STARTED

You certainly may go through this section by yourself. However, we have found it to be very beneficial to assemble a group to work through the exercises together. The most effective groups to work with are those in which you are already a member—at work, in the community, in your faith community, etc. If you decide to do this with a group, make sure that all participants have read through the story in *Red Zone, Blue Zone* prior to beginning.

Make sure that you document the key issues, questions, and concerns that emerge during your own time working through the appendix or in your group discussion.

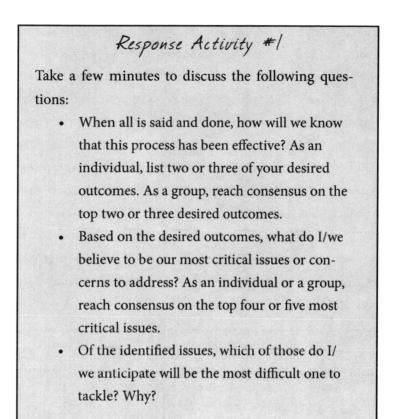

Response Activity #1

Take a few minutes to discuss the following questions:

- When all is said and done, how will we know that this process has been effective? As an individual, list two or three of your desired outcomes. As a group, reach consensus on the top two or three desired outcomes.

- Based on the desired outcomes, what do I/we believe to be our most critical issues or concerns to address? As an individual or a group, reach consensus on the top four or five most critical issues.

- Of the identified issues, which of those do I/we anticipate will be the most difficult one to tackle? Why?

ATTITUDES TOWARD CONFLICT

Let's begin with the attitudes each of us has toward conflict. If we have the wrong attitude toward conflict, it will be impossible to face the emerging conflicts within our lives and deal with them effectively. We realize that the word "conflict" is emotionally loaded. Many people associate conflict with destructive images of people shouting at one another, of gangs shooting at each other, of countries bombing one another. Certainly, those are conflicted situations. But conflict at its core involves disagreement, differing ideas and opinions, and discrepant evaluations and judgments.

People are different. Each person walking this earth has a different slant on things, different ways of seeing what is unfolding, different strategies for dealing with all the situations life throws at us. Issues regarding conflict are confusing. Is conflict good or bad? How do I manage it? Let's put one proposition on the table right up front: conflict is necessary and beneficial—at least, conflict that is focused properly is beneficial (i.e., the Blue Zone conflict, which we will discuss later). As conflict strays away from issues and accesses personal stories (i.e., the Red Zone), conflict becomes unmanageable and destructive.

Response Activity #2

Begin with these questions for yourself or your leadership team:

- Where, in the past, have you thought conflict primarily resided? In others? Between yourself and others? Within yourself?
- Given where you thought the conflict resided, what has been your usual course of action when conflict loomed and unfolded?
- Consider conflicts that have emerged and may continue to emerge in your family. When were conflicts handled poorly? List the elements that led to a poor handling of conflict.

- Consider the conflicts that have troubled your leadership team in the past. When were conflicts handled poorly? List the elements that led to a poor handling of conflict for your team.
- Has there been a general style—an acceptable leadership team style—of dealing with conflict in the past? (Example: As a team, we usually avoid conflict at all costs. Or: We usually end up in the senior leader's office, and she decides who is to blame.)
- Do we as a leadership team have the capacity to raise difficult issues without becoming adversarial?
- What usually happens to the team when difficult issues arise?
- What usually happens to you personally when difficult issues arise?
- What is your influence on the team, and vice versa, as these difficult situations are unfolding? (Example: The team seeks to dive into the situation, which raises my anxiety even higher, and I end up distracting the team.)

In the following sections, we will discuss two attitudes toward conflict: the Blue Zone and the Red Zone. Throughout these discussions, Throughout these discussions, you will see where personal conflict lies and begin exploration into developing healthier attitudes toward conflict.

CHAPTER TEN

THE BLUE ZONE

The Blue Zone is the professional mode of conflict. Here, the focus is on the organization, be it your family, your business or agency, your place of worship, your club, wherever. Blue Zone behavior is focused on the organization's values and mission. We move into the Blue Zone when we focus on underlying issues (even when the underlying issues may be personal). Blue Zone behavior protects the organization rather than the self. Self-interest, in fact, always takes second chair to the organization's mission.

There are actually three critical Blue Zone skills that must be understood and mastered in order for you to forward conflict to a productive conclusion:

1. Questioning and listening
2. Pacing
3. Reframing

Let's look at each one in turn.

QUESTIONING AND LISTENING

Most folks in positions of leadership—parents, coaches, managers, and so on—die with their mouths open. Instead of listening, they're either chattering away or merely keeping silent, waiting for their turn to talk. Leaders who lead from the Blue Zone must know how to listen. Leaders need to want to listen. They must value listening, and they must see listening as a difficult art that must be learned. Of course, the subtext here is the belief that people around you are valuable, that their opinions and disagreements matter. If you don't believe that—which probably means you think your opinion is the only one with merit—then the rest of this will be useless. Valuing others and their opinions sets the foundation for the person firmly situated in the Blue Zone.

Good listening is fueled by curiosity and empathy; it's hard to be a great listener if you're not interested in other people.

Some of the great leaders in the airline business are good examples of listening: Jan Carlzon at SAS (Scandinavian Airlines System) in the early 1980s, Colin Marshall at British Airways in the early 1990s, and Herb Kelleher at Southwest Airlines. These were leaders who were always flying on their own airlines' planes, talking with customers, encouraging ticket agents and baggage handlers, and listening. This active role can be called a "dynamic listening" mode, asking questions all the time. And the great listeners aren't always providing answers. Remember that the trans-formational leader is one who acts more as listener and facilitator, precisely because the stakeholders themselves must wrestle with the competing values.

A warning here: many subordinates (and this includes children in families) when asked a question will remain silent. They've been conditioned in other situations that their opinion is not really sought after. The leader is merely asking a rhetorical question that the leader herself will answer. So you'll need to be patient at first and remind your mentees and direct reports that what they have to say is truly valued.

Once the Blue Zone leader has learned to listen, she must now learn how to ask powerful questions. Powerful questions are important because they draw others into our own thinking, they allow others to express diverse opinions, and they ripen conversations.

POWERFUL QUESTIONS:

- come from a place of genuine curiosity.
- are direct, simple, and usually open-ended.
- generate creative thinking and surface underlying information.
- encourage self-reflection.

Great listeners listen musically as well as analytically.

Jimmy Carter is an example of a president who was "tone deaf." He relied on "rational discourse" to weigh the pros and cons of various initiatives. People prepared papers that he would sift through in private. Doing it that way enabled him to listen to their arguments analytically, but not musically. Jimmy Carter did not enjoy being in meetings where there was posturing, arguing, and haggling. You could say he was conflict-averse. But as we said about great teams, they are loaded with conflict.

We don't have conflict for conflict's sake. All arguments and disagreements give us clues about what people really see is at stake, their values, the subtext that includes the history of the situation, and the personal stakes that people bring to an argument.

Listening musically attunes the leader to the tone of voice and the intensity of the argument which, in turn, point to the underlying concerns. Listening musically enables leaders to get underneath and behind the surface to ask, "What's the real argument that we're having?" And that's a critical question to answer because in the absence of an answer to that question you get superficial buy-in. People go along in a pseudo-consensus, or in a deferential way, but without commitment.

Another thing to remember about listening: grandiosity is the enemy! Leaders need to check their sense of self-importance. This goes hand-in-hand with the sense that "my" perspective is the one true perspective. This can grow into the myth of certainty—that you know exactly what's best in all situations. This doesn't arise from bad intentions. It usually grows out of the normal human need to feel important. We don't know any human being who doesn't want to feel valuable. But unchecked, this desire to feel important can belittle those that the leader ought to be listening to and supporting, even if the leader seems to be solving problems.

The more we demonstrate our capacity to take problems off other people's shoulders, the more authority we gain in their eyes until, finally, we become a senior executive or a CEO. And by then, the tracks have been laid so deeply inside our brain that it becomes hard to stand back, hard to listen, hard to learn from others. Our normal need to feel important—"Let me help you"—has been transformed into grandiosity—"I have all the answers." This, as we already said, is the opposite of the transformational leader.

Now consider these points about active listening. You've probably seen these before, but they're worth repeating (we see these violated over and over again):

1. **Face the speaker.**

2. **Maintain eye contact,** to the degree that you all remain comfortable.

3. **Minimize external distractions.**

4. **Respond appropriately** to show that you understand.

5. **Focus solely on what the speaker is saying.**

6. **Minimize internal distractions.**

7. **Keep an open mind.**

8. **Avoid letting the speaker know how you handled a similar situation.**

9. Even if the speaker is launching a complaint against you, **wait until they finish to defend yourself.**

10. **Ask questions for clarification.** But, once again, wait until the speaker has finished to make sure you didn't misunderstand. Start with: "So you're saying . . . "

Response Activity #3

If you are in a group, discuss the following:

- Describe a person with whom you worked in the past who was an exceptionally good listener. List the specific qualities he demonstrated that let you know he was a good listener.
- Describe a person who was an exceptionally poor listener and describe the qualities that made him a poor listener.

PACING

Blue Zone behavior moves a person to pace the person with whom they are experiencing conflict. Pacing involves getting into the other person's world, seeing things from their perspective, affirming that perspective (though often not agreeing), and demonstrating empathy (through words and nonverbal cues). When we are in conflict with another person, we cannot understand the other person's perspective if our own story and its anxiety have emerged. Our

focus will immediately move from the other person to ourselves, which will compromise our ability to understand not
only the Blue Zone issue at hand but also the other person's
perspective on the issue.

This is not giving the impression of agreement. In fact,
that would be ludicrous and downright manipulative to give
the impression of agreement when in fact you don't agree.
Being understood is one thing. Agreeing is quite another.
But hearing and giving the impression of understanding is
critical.

GETTING IN "SYNC"

When we engage with others, our hands move, our fore-
heads furrow, and our bodies posture. Each of these actions
unconsciously signal particular messages as to how we're
feeling and how our verbal messages are to be understood.

Slow-motion filming of this phenomenon has shown
that there is a "micro synchrony" of small movements, so
sensitive that it is hard to see with the naked eye. These
movements include tiny, momentary dips and nods of the
head, tensing of fingers, stretching of lips, and jerks of the
body that become matched for two people with strong
rapport—they become in "sync." Evidently, the right side
of the brain unconsciously registers the movements of the
other, matches these through similar movements, and registers a feeling of warmth toward the person.

Keep in mind what we said about people who agree and get into "sync" with one another. These are people who trust each other. As a result, they begin to mirror each other's posture, rate of delivery, tone of voice, and so forth. And this is exactly what pacing entails. Pacing involves matching the verbal and nonverbal behaviors of the other person so that that person senses unconsciously that you are in "sync" with her, have entered her world, and truly understand her perspective.

Here's my reality and your reality.

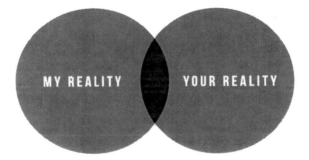

There is some overlap, obviously, in the way the two of us perceive reality. Pacing gives a person the sense that there is significant correlation between my reality and her reality.

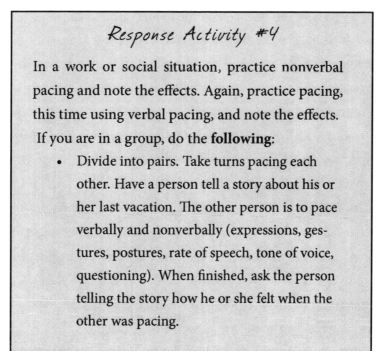

Response Activity #4

In a work or social situation, practice nonverbal pacing and note the effects. Again, practice pacing, this time using verbal pacing, and note the effects. If you are in a group, do the **following:**

- Divide into pairs. Take turns pacing each other. Have a person tell a story about his or her last vacation. The other person is to pace verbally and nonverbally (expressions, gestures, postures, rate of speech, tone of voice, questioning). When finished, ask the person telling the story how he or she felt when the other was pacing.

If you are doing these exercises alone, you can practice with a friend or family member. That person can be enlisted to do the pacing exercise, or you can do it without telling them. During a normal conversation, pace your friend or spouse for a while and note the effect on them. Then, get out of pace with them and note the effect. Afterward, tell them what you were doing and ask how they experienced the exercise.

REFRAMING

Blue Zone behavior also involves reframing problems away from the unsolvable Red Zone (because it's about me) to the underlying issue that is inhibiting performance.

Reframing is one of the most profound and powerful ways to help a person shift perspective and widen his or her map of the world. It has the effect of transforming the meaning of one's experiences. Reframing creates a different context for understanding.

Start with the idea of perspective. Everyone has a perspective on virtually everything. Your perspective on any given situation colors your feelings and informs your actions. Take, for example, an experience where you're home alone at night and you hear footsteps in the house. If your perspective is that it's an intruder, you feel frightened and your actions are to run or grab a weapon. If your perspective is that it's your husband or one of your kids coming in, you feel warm and you prepare for a hug.

The perspective we each bring to our experiences is a function of our development. We all lived a particular story as we grew up. And in that story, we incorporated an infinite number of perspectives that make up our map of reality.

My map of reality is a compilation of all my opinions, assumptions, convictions, values, influences, and experiences. As I grow, my mind attempts to make sense of all it experiences, to interpret any given experience and ascribe meaning and value to it. Remember these two circles?

Here's my perspective on reality, and yours. Note that there's some overlap. If there wasn't, I suppose we wouldn't get anything done. Most people, however, think that there's a total correspondence between their reality and yours. They're frankly dismayed when you didn't like the movie that they thought was sensational.

People operate out of their internal maps. As they encounter new experiences, they take out their map to give them the perspective (or frame) on those experiences. We're directed through all of life using our map to guide us.

Unfortunately, the map is rarely taken out and analyzed. We don't see the map, we see *with* the map, all the while believing that the way we are perceiving the world is universally real. But everyone has a different map of reality. If you are listening to those around you (as recommended above), you'll begin to intuit a person's map of reality in the way they phrase their experiences.

Interestingly, researchers find that the left side of our brains (the logic side) is committed to interpreting all of our overt behavior and emotional responses. Evidently, this is done so that the brain can have a consistent story of all that is happening at any given time. Sometimes the left side will go to bizarre lengths to correlate events into a coherent story. Unfortunately, these explanations from the left side of our brains often contradict the tenets found in the map located on the right side, resulting in incongruence, double messages, and confusion for the listener.

So our perspective or frame (map) helps us to interpret

the meaning of our experiences. But note that our perspective and its usefulness are context bound. In other words, a particular frame that suits us just fine in one context may, in fact, be detrimental in another.

Your job as a Blue Zone leader, when you are in conflict with someone, is to listen carefully to hear how people are framing all of the situations in which you are involved. (You can do this because you are not in the Red Zone and not under the influence of anxiety.) Note to yourself whether these frames are helpful in moving the project, the relationship, and the organization forward. If the frame is not helpful and is miring things down, your job is going to be to reframe the situation so that people can get a different perspective on what is occurring.

You have to first listen carefully in order to pace and gain rapport. Then you must get a sense of the person's perspective (frame) on the issue. Then you need to think of a reframe. All of this—listening, pacing, and reframing—demands that you be in the Blue Zone. If so, you can be a non-anxious presence who is able to focus first yourself and then the other person(s) on the important aspects of the issue at hand.

SUCCESSFUL REFRAMING:

- understands that there is always more than one perspective underlying every problem. Even problematic behavior usually has a positive intention.
- provides an alternative view.
- is valid. This view must make sense and not be just a positive, fanciful notion.
- provides a positive option.
- allows someone to take action.

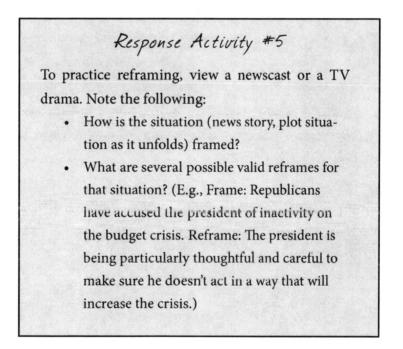

Response Activity #5

To practice reframing, view a newscast or a TV drama. Note the following:

- How is the situation (news story, plot situation as it unfolds) framed?
- What are several possible valid reframes for that situation? (E.g., Frame: Republicans have accused the president of inactivity on the budget crisis. Reframe: The president is being particularly thoughtful and careful to make sure he doesn't act in a way that will increase the crisis.)

BLUE ZONE AS OUR LIFE'S WORK

The Blue Zone allows us to have conflict, even heated conflict, around ideas, values, mission, and strategy. While Red

Zone conflict moves us away from the team, Blue Zone conflict moves us beyond the team to a common purpose. The Blue Zone begins when you becomes aware of your own Red Zone and acknowledges it as your problem.

Creating the Blue Zone is essentially the life work of everyone who aspires to lead a deeply meaningful life. The first step is, of course, the most difficult. It requires that we are completely honest with ourselves and, by extension, honest with those around us in identifying our core issues. The Blue Zone is the willingness to accept responsibility for all our behavior and the consequences of our behavior. It is the continual refusal to shift responsibility for our own actions to any person, to any institution, or to any system.

Awareness of our response sequence helps us to consciously make decisions about our thoughts, feelings, and actions. We are better able to:

- notice our reaction in the conflict.
- identify our core issues being triggered (see below).
- decide on an alternative constructive response.

We can't control what happens to us, but we can choose how to respond. Accepting responsibility for our behavior allows us to change the behavior that is inconsistent with our most personal values. And the inverse is also true. Accepting responsibility for our own behavior protects us from accepting responsibility for others' behavior.

When disagreements arise, the individuals that disagree keep their focus on the mission of the organization and what is ultimately in the best interest of that organization. The exhibited behaviors are:

- thoughtfulness.
- reflectiveness.
- the ability to listen deeply for what the underlying issue might be.
- determination to not see negative intent in the other person(s) who is disagreeing.

CHAPTER ELEVEN

THE RED ZONE

The Red Zone is where the atmosphere is characterized by a lack of professionalism and an abundance of emotional heat. We're not suggesting that Blue Zone conflict that has no emotion. That's absurd. But in the Blue Zone, the emotion is in service of the group because the primary source of the conflict is not emerging from our personal stories, but from the mission of the organization. In the Red Zone, the conflict revolves around the individual: me, my story, my neediness, and my personal issues. The Red Zone emerges from the emotional centers within the brain.

As I sink into the Red Zone, my personal story begins to emerge. That story has a theme or premise that is central to that story: Will I survive? Am I acceptable? Am I competent? Am I in control? As a person begins to sink into the Red Zone, it is usually these same core themes that emerge. Consequently, you will hear these complaints over and over again: *You're trying to control me!* (control) and *Don't you think I can do this?* (competence). This Red Zone theme can color every interaction unless a person becomes aware of the concern and is able to manage it appropriately.

In the Red Zone, the focus becomes personal. Even though we might verbally be disagreeing about an issue involving the organization, the real energy is coming from a personal place. The main focus is not furthering the mission of the organization, but self-protection. Behaviors in evidence are:

- I disengage
- I distract
- I become easily annoyed
- I am resentful
- I procrastinate
- I attack someone personally
- I use alcohol as medication
- I avoid people and situations

Response Activity #6

Note which of the above behaviors you might have employed when you became Red Zone. Add to the list any behaviors not listed here that you might have used.

RED ZONE THEMES

The Red Zone tends to elicit one of four themes: survival, acceptance, control, or competence. As the Red Zone core theme is activated, the feelings associated with that issue are also activated. The person then sinks deeper into a morass of feelings, many of which come from stories completely unrelated to the current situation that has provoked the Red Zone response.

Survival. "I must take care of myself. The world is full of peril, so I must enjoy the moment." These people often grew up in very dysfunctional homes where their caregivers (usually parents) were inconsistent, unavailable, or abusive. Because of their early environment, these people were thrown onto their own resources rather than those of others. These people have traits of competence, self-reliance, and responsibility. These people lack the ability to trust others and tend to be wary and troubled in relationships. They may have little interest in anything but what is of practical benefit. They become angry and panicky (Red Zone) whenever they feel their survival has been threatened.

Acceptance. "I will do anything to be loved and accepted by others. I am a people-pleaser." These people have a heart for serving others and are very attentive to the needs and feelings of other people. These people can be overly compliant and self-effacing. They tend to be rescuers. They become angry and carry personal grudges (Red Zone) whenever they feel they have been rejected. But they can also read people and situations very well.

Control. "The world is a threatening place, and the only way I can feel safe is if I can control every situation and the people around me." These people tend to have strong leadership qualities. They are vigilant, highly organized, and have high expectations of themselves. These people often wall themselves off emotionally. They do not let others get too close to them. They can be overly controlling toward others—bossy, directive, demanding, rigid, and nit-picky. They impose perfectionist demands on others. They become anxious and angry (Red Zone) whenever anyone or anything threatens their control. Though they make good leaders, they can often be poor followers.

Competence. "I am loved only on the basis of my performance. My performance is never good enough, so I never feel worthy of being loved." These people tend to be high achievers. If you are a leader, you want these people on your team, because they will work hard to achieve a great performance. They are never satisfied with their achievements. They have a hard time receiving affirmation from other people. They impose perfectionist demands on themselves. They are defensive and easily angered (Red Zone) whenever they perceive that their competence has been questioned.

Red Zone feelings become more prominent than the ability to think clearly. As a result, the person carries on the conflict, immersed in her own story and the feelings associated with it. This colors her actions and reactions. The ability to clearly understand the issues involved in the conflict are compromised.

Response Activity #7

Write down your core Red Zone issue as you understand it and how it affects you personally. Note that everyone can experience all four themes, but one theme usually stands out as the dominant or signature theme, the other three subordinating to that theme.

YOUR CORE ISSUES	YOUR THOUGHTS AND BEHAVIORS THAT FLOW FROM THE ISSUE	THE RESULTS OF THESE THOUGHTS AND BEHAVIORS
Ex. My core issues is acceptance.	I'm always trying to be the nice guy so I'm loved.	I can never hold people accountable, fearing they won't like me anymore.

If you are doing the exercises in a group, share with the group your own Red Zone issue.

- Now think of the ways you have generally handled conflict. It may be stylized (one size fits all). E.g., "I always back down and acquiesce." "I usually go on the attack."
- Are we willing to consider a new way of handling conflict? Discuss how the team can be helpful to each other in this regard.
- Do the roles and expectations of team members clearly support the unfolding mission of the organization in a concerted way?
- Are performance evaluations clearly tied to roles and expectations in concrete, behavioral ways?

COMMUNICATION AND THE RED ZONE

Part of the problem with the Red Zone has to do with communication. Communication is multi-channeled, and therein lies the problem. I speak words, but I also convey information nonverbally through tone of voice, posture, facial expression, etc. The verbal messages emerge from the intellectual centers of the brain where logic reigns. The nonverbal messages emerge from the emotional centers where my story resides. Notice in the drawing below how these messages are sent.

Notice that the person on the left is saying something to the person on the right. He has a particular intent: "John, would you put that box over here?" Hopefully what he intends by the message equals the impact of his message on John. But that isn't always the case. That's because communication has more than one channel. *What* I say also carries relational signals in the *way* that I say things—body language, tone of voice, facial expressions.

The *way* of the message emerges from the part of the brain that contains my story and the central theme of that story. So let's say my central theme is acceptance, and I want John to move a box. The way I say that to John will undoubtedly be different than if my central theme is control. The Acceptance person quite possibly will have more of a placating manner in her voice as she makes the request. The Control person could have a demanding nonverbal message as she asks John to move the box.

When I say something to you, my words carry one message that you hear consciously (the *what* of my message), while my body language communicates another message (the *way* of my message) which is communicated by me and registered by you unconsciously. What that means is that I can say one thing ("I really value women and their contribution in the workplace") and at the same time contradict that message by my body language (*I never seek out women for their opinions and tend to only hear and value contributions by men. Women can be pushy, and I'm into control.*). Whenever there is a discrepancy between what I say verbally and how I act nonverbally (a double message), the verbal message is rejected. Also, trust in the communicator is diminished or destroyed. *You say that you value women, but your actions don't support that notion.*

I might think that what I'm saying to you is coming across quite logically in the Blue Zone, but my nonverbal messages may convey a completely different message to you: that I am, in fact, in the Red Zone. I'm in conflict with you over what I thought was the mission of our organization. But I have slipped into the Red Zone, and my actions and nonverbal cues betray that fact to you.

POSTURES

As I sink into the Red Zone, I will assume a stylized posture, which becomes part of my nonverbal communication. Often this posture conceals the fact that I am in the Red Zone (e.g., computing looks hyper-reasonable). Take a look at the graph below.

POSTURE	HOPED FOR RESULTS
PLACATING	Often used by Acceptance people. So others won't be mad. "Spare me."
BLAMING	Often used by Control people. So others will see me as strong. "Obey me."
COMPUTING	Often used by Survival people. So others will see I'm not threatened. "Ally with me."
DISTRACTING	Often used by Competence people. So others will ignore the threat. "Tolerate me."

Adapted from Virginia Satir, *Peoplemaking*. (Palo Alto: Science and Behavior, 1972).

Response Activity #8

If you are working through these discussions alone, think of the predominate posture you assume when you slip into the Red Zone during conflict. If you are working in a group, discuss with the team the various postures each of you use and experience as things begin to turn Red Zone. It is most helpful to think of concrete examples of conflict that turned Red Zone. It's usually easier to spot this initially in other people than in yourself. But hopefully as you become more aware of yourself, you'll be able to see how you sink into these unhelpful postures.

BOUNDARIES

Healthy boundaries identify and separate the self from others and consequently are the foundation of the Blue Zone. Boundaries are the fences, both physical and emotional, that mark off our world, creating zones of safety, authority, privacy, and territoriality. Boundaries are essential components because they fulfill many functions:

- they define who we are—what we believe, think, feel, and do—and where my story ends and yours begins;
- they restrict access and intrusions;
- they protect priorities; and
- they differentiate between personal (Red Zone) and professional (Blue Zone) issues.

Boundary difficulties go hand-in-hand with Red Zone issues. As I sink deeper into the morass of the Red Zone, my personal boundaries invariably become involved and compromised, and I engage others in my emotional drama in unhealthy ways.

For some people, boundaries become too rigid. Vital information—the lifeblood of any healthy person—is greatly restricted. Stylized ways of behaving become fixed.

Prejudices are constructed and maintained. These folks often refuse to allow others on their teams who might put forward conflicting information that could be useful in ripening the conversation.

For other people, boundaries become too porous or ambiguous. In such cases, the integrity and cohesion of the person is threatened by a lack of definition—"Who am I, other than an extension of you?"

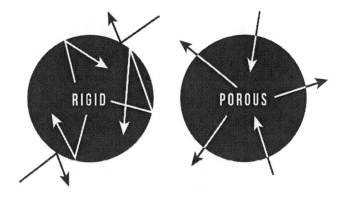

Those with porous boundaries are usually the ones who are most noticeably in the Red Zone. They are the ones who seem to be constantly influenced by what others do, say, and think. But those with too-rigid boundaries can be just as influenced by the Red Zone. They've just constructed higher and denser walls to keep out external influences because of their feelings (Red Zone) of vulnerability.

We are used to the visible boundary markers of our world: fences, hedges, traffic signs. Less obvious, but equally effective, are the internal boundaries that mark off emotional territory: "These are my thoughts, my feelings, my story," or "This is my responsibility, not yours." These internal boundaries are emotional barriers that protect and enhance the integrity of individuals.

Boundaries are critical in understanding the Red Zone because, as we have said, sinking into the Red Zone represents a boundary violation. When I am in conflict with another person, it is critical that my thoughts and emotions stay present to the issues upon which we disagree. When I permit old storylines to creep into the equation and color my feelings, I have violated a boundary and I have compromised my thinking. When I begin to see another person as someone other than who she truly is, I violate a boundary. For people who have poor boundaries (too rigid or too porous), the dangers of Red-Zoning are all the more prominent.

Response Activity #9

Here's a quick test to help you determine the strength and health of your own personal boundaries (based on ideas suggested by C. L. Whitfield in *Boundaries and Relationships* and also used in *Thriving Through Ministry Conflict*. See if you agree or disagree with the following statements:

Agree	*Disagree*	
		I have difficulty making up my mind.
		I have difficulty saying "no" to people.
		I feel my happiness depends on other people.
		I would rather attend to others than myself.
		Others' opinions are more important than mine.
		People take and use my things without asking me.

		I have difficulty asking for what I want or need.
		I would rather go along with other people than express what I would really like to to.
		It's hard for me to know what I think and believe.
		I have a hard time determining what I feel.
		I don't get to spend much time alone.
		I have a hard time keeping a confidence.
		I am very sensitive to criticism.
		I tend to stay in relationships that are harmful to me.
		I tend to take on or feel what others are feeling.
		I feel responsible for other people's feelings.

If you answered "agree" to three or more of these, your boundaries are too porous, with beliefs, information, values, and opinions flowing freely in and out without a clear definition of self.

Now look at this list and see which ones agree with you.

Agree	Disagree	
		My mind is always made up.
		It is much easier for me to say "no" to people than to say "yes."
		My happiness never depends on other people.

		I would rather attend to myself than to others.
		My opinion is more important than others'.
		I rarely, if ever, lend my things to other people.
		Most issues appear very black-and-white to me.
		I know exactly what I think and believe on almost every issue.
		I spend much time alone.
		I keep most of my thoughts to myself.
		I am immune to criticism.
		I find it difficult to make and maintain close relationships.
		I never feel responsible for other people's feelings.

If you answered "agree" to more than three of these, your boundaries are probably too rigid. Yes, too rigid. You might think that agreeing with many of the above statements gives you good, strong boundaries. But boundaries must be permeable enough to allow new information to enter and to influence you in useful ways.

STEPS TO CREATING HEALTHY INTERNAL BOUNDARIES:

- Learn to recognize your own emotional responses.
- Become aware of when you are reacting to an authority figure, a peer, or a situation.

- Become aware when the other person is reacting to something in you.
- Recognize situations in which you repeat the same behavior and produce the same result.
- Recognize situations that create anxiety for you, and acknowledge that fear to yourself.
- When a conflict arises, talk about your behavior and feelings with someone. Avoid focusing on the other person's behavior.
- Become aware of the people who provoke emotional responses in you. Identify the characteristics in that person that provoke the emotional response in you. (E.g., He is so arrogant or so needy or so angry.)
- Recognize that if you are unable to resolve an issue with someone after talking about it, then there is another deeper-level conflict present. If you realize that another issue is present, acknowledge it and get support from a third party.

STEPS TO CREATING HEALTHY EXTERNAL BOUNDARIES:

- Understand your target audience, and anticipate what the resistance will be.
- When you experience resistance from others, avoid personalizing the situation.
- Ask questions in a non-threatening manner, and genuinely seek to understand the issues.
- Do not respond in the moment if you are feeling threatened.

- Recognize that organizational blind spots are just that—
  blind spots. There is no intent to do wrong if people are not
  aware of the consequences of their actions.
- Determine when you need help, what kind, and how
  much.
- Create a safe environment.
- Be aware of team values when you feel attacked from the
  outside.
- Don't assume that the same things work for everyone.
- Give feedback.
- Share information.
- Ask for help.
- Have agreed-upon values and expectations.
- Create more clarity around task and purpose.
- Create more clarity around roles and responsibility.
- Have an understanding and tolerance for various work
  styles.
- Be better at giving and receiving feedback.
- Show support for each other.
- Look for people who have insight into your audience.
- Value and reinforce the work we do as an organization for
  the organization.

CHAPTER TWELVE

THE SAME PEOPLE KEEP SHOWING UP IN MY LIFE

This is a hard concept for many people to grasp, so let's walk through it. When we are growing up, certain people, beginning with our primary caregivers, carve an indelible impression on our brains and in our personal stories. Each of these important people has distinct characteristics that influence us. These can be positive and negative. The kindly grandmother imprints characteristics of love, acceptance, and nurturing. The overbearing father imprints control, disapproval, and non-acceptability. These characteristics remain buried in our stories in our emotional brains but are summoned later in life as we encounter people who remind us in some way of that primary person who first influenced us. And that reminder is often minimal (e.g., my boss is nothing like my overbearing father, but he is in a position of authority over me, and that's enough to activate dad's characteristics).

When I meet a person later in life who reminds me of the primary person who imprinted on my brain, I place on that person (i.e., I project) the characteristics of the primary person. When I meet an older woman with a certain smile, I place on her the characteristics of my loving grandmother and then expect her to act in a similar way. When I meet the boss who can be gruff at times, I place on him all of the characteristics of my overbearing father and act toward him in ways similar to how I acted toward my father, all the while expecting him to be that father-person I imagined.

Our minds also play tricks on us. Once the primary characteristics have been projected, our minds only see in the other person those actions and behaviors that confirm our suspicions that this new person is just like the primary person. In other words, when my "overbearing" boss acts kindly toward me, I just might dismiss or ignore that behavior. I filter out the good in my boss, seeing only those behaviors that confirm what I have already made him out to be.

These primary people, the good ones and the bad ones, keep showing up. You might be saying, "This sounds a lot like prejudice," and you're right. Prejudice has to do with pre-judging another person before you really get to know

them. And once the judgment is made, it is often very difficult to disconfirm what we have already judged about that
other person because, as we said, our minds censor out dis-
confirming data and only allow that data which confirms
our pre-judgment.

Response Activity #10

Now take some time to fill out the chart below.
Note those people who had the most influence in
shaping who you are (for good or ill) when you
were growing up. Pay special attention to the fourth
column where you have to discern characteristics
that you tend to miss about each person.

VERY INFLUENCIAL PEOPLE	MOST IMPORTANT CHARACTER-ISTICS	PEOPLE TODAY WHO EXHIBIT THE SAME CHARACTERIS-TICS	OTHER CHAR-ACTERISTICS I TEND TO IGNORE
Sample: Mother	warm, loving, accepting, non-judgemental	Susie, Mr. Jones, Mrs. Smith	Susie is a gossip

RESISTANCE IS YOUR ALLY

Call it what you will—resistance, pushback, challenge, opposition—it's basically an opposing force that slows or stops movement. Anyone in leadership, be it parenting, teaching, directing government agencies or multinational corporations, should come to expect resistance. It is ubiquitous. It is important to *not* be surprised when resistance emerges. In fact, it is an element in the process that should be welcomed. Welcome it, then learn to handle it correctly.

All of us, from time to time, resist. It's a way of protecting ourselves from real or perceived danger, most notably when change is unfolding. In and of itself, resistance is not a bad thing. It's merely energy. If we can effectively redirect that energy, we can move the resistance in the direction of change.

The first signal resistance sends to our mind is *I don't like this change. In fact, I don't like* any *change.* The second thing resistance signals is *Okay, I can tolerate some change, but you're going too fast!* When the signal inside of us activates, it is up to us to figure out what the signal means. The same principle applies when your smoke detector goes off in your house late at night. You can say to yourself, "Darn smoke detector," while you rip it off the wall and destroy it. Or you can try to figure out what the detector is signaling to you. If there's a fire, you surely want to know about it.

Resistance tends to signal that issues lurk under the surface and are tapping into our deepest-held values (what we call transformational or adaptive issues). That's one of the great benefits of resistance. It's the most effective signal for the presence of these core transformational issues. What we find over and over is that people apply tactical solutions to transformational problems. And that never works. So when you apply a tactical solution and the resistance continues, or the solution becomes the problem, that should tell you that transformational issues are lurking somewhere in the bushes. For further information on this idea, the book *The Leadership Triangle* by Kevin Ford and Ken Tucker more fully explains these issues and what to do about them.

Most people don't recognize and adapt to a transformational change. They end up butting their heads against the resistance instead of listening to the signal, intuiting what it is saying, and deciding what to do next. Your job as a leader is to find themes and possibilities. You've got to be able to stay Blue Zone and realize it's not about you; it's about the mission. Once that perspective is put into place, you'll be able to respect those who resist and use the energy resistance generates to increase your success.

Response Activity #11

Here's a quiz that should help point out some of those internal areas that might still be tripping you up.

- What things really set me off and cause me to overreact?
- Do I read other people's minds? Whose? When do I read them? What is occurring?
- What do I fear the most? Rejection? Loss of control? Incompetence? Abandonment?
- What people or things do I hate the most?
- What characteristics do I find myself disliking in others (especially those of the same sex)? Is there one person in my life that I really can't stand? What is it about him or her; what characteristics set me off?
- What things do I know about myself that I try hard to keep hidden, even from those closest to me?
- What things do I *never* do, even though doing them may benefit me?
- What "strengths" do I have that, when preoccupied with them, may prevent me from being real and having fulfilling relationships (e.g., always taking care of others prevents me caring for myself)?

- What are the themes of my dreams? Who is doing what?
- What do others say about me, especially those closest to me (spouse, friends, parents)? How am I perceived in my organization?
- Think back on a recent hardship, a loss of something truly important to you (spouse, friendship, job, status). What issues emerged? What was said to you?

Remember, when it comes to resistance:

- It is an expected part of change.
- Progress without resistance is impossible.
- We resist change that we perceive will be harmful (e.g., when we start losing weight, our body slows our metabolism, fearing starvation).
- Resistance alerts us to particular dynamics that are going on at the moment.

Response Activity #12

Reflection Scenario: If you are doing these exercises with a group, brainstorm among team members about when there has been a significant initiative (it may be a current initiative, or one from the past), preferably an initiative that brewed controversy within the team and/or within the organization. Select from those generated one initiative and its controversy that is most representative of other similar incidents. Reflect on who was involved, what the issue(s) was, and how you as a team mobilized to meet the controversy.

Reflection Questions:

1. How did you try to defuse the situation (e.g., controlling the conversation, making deals, killing the messenger)?

2. What toll did this take on you personally? In your family? On the team?

3. To date, have there been any lessons that team members have learned about the nature of resistance and how it can best be handled?

Resistance can take on many guises (adapted from Rick Maurer's *Beyond the Wall of Resistance*):

- **Confusion.** "So why are we doing this (after many explanations)?"

- **Immediate criticism.** "What a dumb idea."
- **Denial.** "I don't see any problem here."
- **Malicious compliance.** "I concur completely and wholeheartedly."
- **Sabotage.** "Let's get him!"
- **Easy agreement.** "No problem."
- **Deflection.** "What do you think the Cubs' chances are this year?"
- **Silence.**
- **In-your-face criticism.** "You're the worst leader we've ever had!"

When faced with resistance, we can act in one of two ways: reaction in the Red Zone or action in the Blue Zone. When we react in the Red Zone, we first assume that the resistance is about us personally ("Why doesn't he like what I'm proposing? Does he think I'm incompetent?"), not about our roles. Feeling personally attacked, we then use a number of maneuvers.

When we're in the Blue Zone, we can welcome the resistance as a normal part of forward movement, seek to understand it and the underlying issues generating it, and work to be effective with those who are creating the resistance.

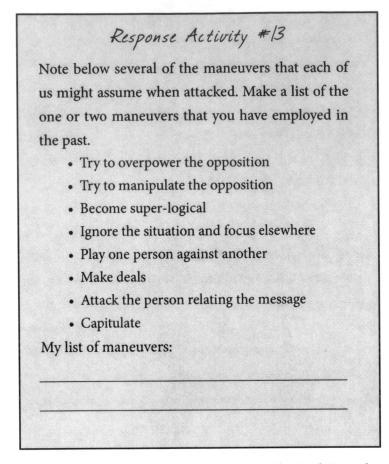

Response Activity #13

Note below several of the maneuvers that each of us might assume when attacked. Make a list of the one or two maneuvers that you have employed in the past.

- Try to overpower the opposition
- Try to manipulate the opposition
- Become super-logical
- Ignore the situation and focus elsewhere
- Play one person against another
- Make deals
- Attack the person relating the message
- Capitulate

My list of maneuvers:

_____

_____

You can be well aware that you're in the Red Zone by your responses when:

- they increase, rather than decrease, resistance.
- they fail to create synergy.
- they create fear and suspicion.
- they separate us from others.

So what to do? Remember, you must be in the Blue Zone, and that involves several aspects of control:

- Maintain clear focus
- Manage your fears
- Embrace resistance (remember, it's your ally!)
- Respect those who resist
- Join with the resistance

Now revisit the original issue generated above that troubled the leadership team. Discuss with the leadership team how to implement these suggestions.

ABOUT THE AUTHORS

JAMES OSTERHAUS (PhD, American University) is a founding partner and consultant for TAG. A psychologist and executive coach, James has authored numerous books and is called upon to speak around the world.

JOSEPH JURKOWSKI (MA, University of Maryland) is the leader and a founding partner of TAG. He has worked with Fortune 500 companies and organizations of all kinds as a strategic thinker and partner. He is one of the most respected consultants working with the federal government.

TODD HAHN (M.Div., Gordon-Conwell Theological Seminary) serves as a consultant with TAG and is also a church pastor. The author or coauthor of six previous books, Todd is recognized as a dynamic speaker and a consultant who brings clarity to organizational direction. His recent book, *Your Intentional Difference: One Word Changes Everything* (coauthored with Ken Tucker and Shane Roberson) was an Amazon Business Bestseller.

ABOUT FAMILIUS

Welcome to a place where mothers are celebrated, not compared. Where heart is at the center of our families, and family at the center of our homes. Where boo boos are still kissed, cake beaters are still licked, and mistakes are still okay. Welcome to a place where books—and family—are beautiful. Familius: a book publisher dedicated to helping families be happy.

VISIT OUR WEBSITE: WWW.FAMILIUS.COM

Our website is a different kind of place. Get inspired, read articles, discover books, watch videos, connect with our family experts, download books and apps and audiobooks, and along the way, discover how values and happy family life go together.

JOIN OUR FAMILY

There are lots of ways to connect with us! Subscribe to our newsletters at www.familius.com to receive uplifting daily inspiration, essays from our Pater Familius, a free ebook every month, and the first word on special discounts and Familius news.

BECOME AN EXPERT

Familius authors and other established writers interested in helping families be happy are invited to join our family and contribute online content. If you have something important to say on the family, join our expert community by applying at:

www.familius.com/apply-to-become-a-familius-expert

GET BULK DISCOUNTS

If you feel a few friends and family might benefit from what you've read, let us know and we'll be happy to provide you with quantity discounts. Simply email us at specialorders@familius.com.

Website: www.familius.com

Facebook: www.facebook.com/paterfamilius

Twitter: @familiustalk, @paterfamilius1

Pinterest: www.pinterest.com/familius

The most important work you ever do will be within the walls of your own home.

CPSIA information can be obtained
at www.ICGtesting.com
Printed in the USA
FSOW02n1536170315
5789FS